BURN-OUT

Cover Photo: In the stormy, heat-laden summer of 2022, France burned under hundred-degree temperatures and the sky moved from intense sunshine to brooding clouds which refused to surrender their rain. Photo by the author, image edited by his son Peter [echophotographics.com], was taken mid-July in the Marais facing south into Paris and the Left Bank.

BURN-OUT

Stephen M. Honig

To the poet known as Choo.

Index

2 ABOUT MY WOMEN

3 ABOUT PAIN

Burn–Out

After four years reading everything about politics and our future
    I declare a personal time-out.
I am going to read poems and old novels.
I am going to re-open those books by Galsworthy which have
    as frontispiece a three-page fold-out of a fictional family tree.
I am going to care again about the Boston Red Sox and find
    someone who will bet on their end-of-season standing.
I am going to think about sex and rock and roll,
    and wonder how I have for decades missed the drug part.
I am going to find a dark hill, brave the cold, replace the batteries
    in my tracking telescope,
    and find some planets and transit some stars.
I am going to pretend I live in Banff, and that the road to the
    U.S. border has been closed permanently due to repairs
    which are not intended.

(From a text email to friends sent two days after President Biden's swearing in)

1

ABOUT MYSELF

Myself is much confused. Thus also my poetry about myself. If you seek certainty, do not read Section 1.

Memory of Objects

Never clean your storage
unless you are prepared to engage the memory of objects.
You will tell me that things have no memory
and that the memory is in the eye of the holder,
a trigger of recognition emotion melancholy
of a person moment epiphany death—
such is the insistence of logic
imposing will on wonder.

Here is a toy my son played with in his bathtub
splashing and swooping this small yellow duck
and warm water and bubbles are described to me.
Here is a sweater I wore when I was newly married
telling me with a smile I cannot get into it now.
Here is a comb, amber plastic with long fingers,
that entwined my first wife's red hair before it grayed
and fell to earth at the hands of medicine, reminding me
of fine strands of soft whimsy.
Here is a baseball glove recounting that grab of a line drive
July 4 picnic 1957 and is that leather mitt still proud!

Be fearful, though, of the date of things:
    dates are without their own memory
but jolts of age slapping you:
could it have been 60 years ago,
how old was I then
how old now
how long to remember—
I will need the objects to tell me who I was
before I am myself.

There is a brass match box
in the shape of a shoe,
small and with a hinged lid where the tiny foot would go,
it traveled in my mother's mother's sack
from Russia when one of those Presidents you
    never know anything about
who was after Grant was it Hayes who can recall
and it reminds me that it was not seasick
and lit many a wood stove fire on the farm before the
    Great Depression
and sat on a tenement window sill when my mother
    took it with her
running to the city, a young girl in search of her tomorrow
carrying her yesterday with her as an ornament;
now sitting on a shelf in a corner book-case stuck in a back room
anxious to stir itself and tell me its journey.
Some things are so old that they are tired of telling their stories
but they are compelled.

No one ever believes me when I tell them that my objects
    have memories
within their brittle atoms
suspended droplets of minutes and soul
coming out to frolic or complain
when someone holds them.
They laugh, these objects, at the conceit that it is the holder
    with the thoughts.
They know better
and more than you know, so
—be careful when you choose to clean your closets basements
    attics back rooms.
You may be silent, but you are asking for a dialog with time.

THE KEYS OF APRIL

I had an invitation from spring
but in late April it was withdrawn.
blue flowers piercing through dead leaves
lied to me about my prospects.
robins must have gone back South.

what new can be said about Aprils,
pro or con?
the sun is high in New England,
wind coldly fickle.
rain lurks in pregnant clouds.

many head South when Winter comes
but I do not.
I embrace weather if I see it coming.
Spring is a promise with a low neckline,
all décolletage, no decorum.

I seek the steam of Key West,
sitting itself on brittle shells and rocks,
beer dousing languor, as April births into May.
then my feet stand in shallow tides
and report upwards that all is well.

I am stared at in my jeans and dress shirt
as rolled cuffs and sleeves do not a native make.
I must reek of Northern pine
frozen into interstices of clothing;
no overlay of nonchalance can fool my bartender.

you may think escape to drink
and off-loading emotion in the ocean
is indulgence that prudence eschews
but for me, the breeze in the Keys
releases desires and kindles warm fires—
indulgence with nothing to lose.

Three Mornings in June, 2021

1. We were elated beyond control
grinning ear to ear
and beyond, our smiles
wrapped around our heads so even those behind us
were forced to grin in concert.
We held good will to all
refused to hear complaint
lip-smacked icing on the cake of the world
and slept while music fell from the stars.
We awoke with fires in intestines and behind our eyes
and were prepared to continue to exult
but the engine of self-pride had abandoned us,
leaving us without the mechanics of pleasure,
without the confidence to enjoy the mirror before us.
To think about the slide from the mountain
requires thinking about the value of the view from the peak,
its purported vantage point as high and thus justified
    and virtuous,
its nature, whether pinnacle or tor or mesa or alp, as both worthy
    and earned
—but then, why are we next morning looking upwards,
    fallen from joy,
smelling the swamp gas of today?
I know you from before, your eye drew mine into the interstices
    of time and space
and danced with confident light.

Do you know how we have failed?
Is it occasion or core, happenstance or weakness,
 an isolated accident of life or a life of accidents?
I reach out for your hand, then,
in search of warmth and a passing pressure of affirmation.
Your palm bears the cold sweat of shared dejection
here in the valley of truth.

2. The bird outside at 4 am
sees over the rim
and feels the bent rays of warmth
delivered to feather and crest by curving electrons
shaped by gravity into dawn.
In my bed, the sense of impending light might be beaten back, but
    this bird is herald not to be denied.
I do not know if this bird is dark or bright,
girl or boy
fresh out of robin-blue wrapper
or wizened by hawks and recalcitrant insects,
believing it is helping to arouse me to just pursuit
or seducing me to luxury which at dusk I will call waste.
This bird is as cryptic as the coming day,
revealing nothing except its arrival,
promising the flatness of nothing
or the ascendancy of victory
or the misery of death or—
even worse—the trumpet call of death,
itself on the cusp of a morning
when flower will awaken,
but you shall not...

3. They are building structures around me,
of wood and brick and board and nails
of hammers and drills and the dull thud of pallets dropping on
    the earth.
There are shudders in the walls
echoes around the thin curtains
voices of people at labor
beeps of machines heading backwards
all playing against the guilt of the covers under which I coil.
Purpose is afoot while I am abed,
and I take offense that my sloth should be called out,
anonymously, callously, continually, and finally
successfully.
I arise uncurled, step lumbering and barefoot in the carpet's
    ill-gained grit
and descend stairs to find coffee pot
and my future.

Fireplace in Winter

it is
finally
cold
cold enough to make fires again
and so I am carrying logs indoors
piling them to the right of the hearth
in irregular stacks of yellows and browns.
the iron rack
black and sturdy
bears its load in expectation of many visits now that the sun
    is low to the horizon.
the logs are dried in the garage
and supplemented by a resupply from the lovely young man
    with beard and plaid
who promised to only bring the well-dried pieces
in apology for last year when his wood
crackled and spit water when put to the match.
My fingers have those small black lines under the skin
where the bark has managed to intrude
and the small blond lines finer still
where the wood itself has found a warm home out of the fire.
I will soak my fingers tonight
and take a needle then
its tip sterilized by match
and pick and poke and pull
until I no longer feel the pang and pressure in my palm
of vagabond shards stowing away in my hands.
My feet will cozy up to the fire screen
and twitch their toes in harmony with the logs' surrender
and the crackle will find a rhythm
while I nod and let my chin fall onto my chest.
Then, I will counterpoint the forest beat
with sounds of my sleeping smile.

First Draft of a Poem About October 13, 2021

1. The Day
Autumn falls with the warmth of summer.
Baseball scores as it is devoid of politics.
Squirrels are chewing shallow white strips in the skin of my
    front porch pumpkin.
Who am I when the West wind blows?
Dawn was dark, the sun not yet ascendant.
Where are my children,
spread across America and all in pain?
I plan today to skip tomorrow
as harbingers arrive on an ill tide.

2. The Job
Only a few people, some new and unknown
and shielded from being known by mask and averted eyes.
They have fired my assistant and have failed to tell me.
My revenges are twofold:
I do no work
and steal a handful of blue pens as I pass through the door.

3. The Bar
In the wood-paneled room
women in low-cut black dresses and pearls.
"I'll have a 'Gansett.'"
My beer arrives with a shallow bowl of pallid dry-roasted nuts.
The stool to my right pivots and I am asked
"Are you waiting for someone?"
With lowered lids I sigh "Who isn't?"
No doubt the wrong tone, she swivels away from me.

4. The Night at Home
The owl in my tree is silent
and I do not give a hoot.
Lyricism defers to cynicism, while
down the street,
five turkeys are asleep on a neighbor's lawn.

5. The Philosophical Detritus of the Day
This is a life, so-called
frozen in time but without purpose.
If you were me, what would you say?
Or, would the cat get your tongue,
its whiskers twitching silently in the night?

January 29, 2022 @ 5:35 pm
in Newton, Massachusetts

I have been waiting all last night, and all today;
the sun has no doubt set, somewhere behind the
   clouds and snow,
blown over the Western brim by the blizzard winds.
Snow blocks my windows, clinging to the screens,
blocks my walkways, not that I have anywhere to go
but also blocks my dog, timid in white powder
   taller than he is—
we have dug a path for him, dug an open area in the yard,
and each hour go back outside to redig his pathway
so that he does not burst apart or do his business on our floor.
We have done for dog what we would not do for ourselves,
we trap ourselves but not our dog for whom
   we feel deep empathy.
There are times we have cursed him and his foibles
barks, diggings, droppings, sheddings, emanations
thefts of food, chaws of stocking
eating holes in furniture and chewing out pockets of clothing
but something in the snowtime makes us kinder—
today we call him "puppy" and not "that sonofabitch"
and he in his eleventh dog year.
I said I am still waiting.
Snow is piled on our outdoor table, it must be almost
   two feet high
a pure geometry, even sloped sides, a glaze or sheen
   reflecting our porch light,
staring back at us through a veil of fine flakes.
The men will come, first with plows for the garage and
only later
much later for the walkways.

The dog gets dug out first the cars second; we are third
and only we receive the bill.
Our son left for college with a few Christmas bulbs
    hanging on high tree limbs.
Today they have caps of snow
except for those which, weighted down,
have fallen into the powder, hidden now until the melting time.
We will find red and green and golden tinkly shards
    of colored balls
mixed in with the melt, to be picked carefully
    out of the tight early Spring grass
when the melting is done with its work.
We are waiting still and by now you are wondering:
what are they waiting for?
We are waiting for the lesson embodied in the tired old aphorism:
"If you don't like the New England weather, wait a minute…"
I have waited enough. I am balancing small logs on large logs,
rolling old newspapers and topping them with kindling,
dishonoring equally the lowly comics of the Boston Globe
and all that was fit to print of the New York Times
and the homey hoo-ie of the town weekly
all burned as witches in the same auto-de-fé
all pushing out into the wind from our chimney
to frolic with wood smoke and blasts from the plains
and soaking molecules from the Gulf
ashes to ashes but fires to the wind
and there is red wine and smelly cheese
and agave tequila pale and reposado
lauding its purity
loathing the smokey Mezcal as only the smoke
    of the fireplace is recognized today.

We will play card games
watch bad movies,
hear the same tired announcers announce
    the advancing snow pack
with an urgency as if we care about an extra two or six inches
because it's a goddamned blizzard, ya hear?
deep enough so that you do not care about
    its precise dimensions.

At last, something that is not a virus is locking us indoors,
    away from people.
The weather has snowed us!
We feel wholly fulfilled,
stuffed with joy and warmth,
and while you are up
please bring back some limes and salt.

WEATHER REPORT

I waited for a rainy morning
mist on the hill, drizzle playing taps on tin roof
to tell her I was leaving.
moods are important.
West of Boston
the car wanted to turn around
and I had to fight the instinct.
when sun cracked the floating gray shroud
I pressed onward faster, but
it is hard to drive with sunlight refracted through tears.

Ahead, a rainbow invited me into dark of night…

A POEM FOR MY FAMILY AND FRIENDS FOR DECEMBER 24TH 2021

It's Christmas
and we have a tree
with lights
ornaments
and a broken crown on top
passed down through years of family catastrophe
falling tree
dropped decoration
unknown damage when the box is opened for the coming year.
The ornaments too are a mixed bag; some bear initials on the back
and year of construction
and they hang although some of the craftsmen
are no longer with us, their memories for a blessing.
I carefully hang some ceramics roughly hewn by
    my wife of decades
dated when she was not yet ten
when the makers of our family ornaments were children too
when the crown atop our tree was whole, with tingling bells
when the world was young
when Santa, not quite real, was not yet an embarrassing thought.
I hang ornaments we bought as a family
my son in college now but then
when ornaments of hobby horses and trains and soldiers
    were appealing to the eye.
I hang ornaments cataloging our first Christmas
our fifth Christmas
Christmases now long past
and remembered only as a whole body of Christmases
reeking pine and pain, pangs and promises
love shared and loved betrayed
life spent like sand flowing through my hand into the ocean

lost in the tides and flow.
Our tree is tall
and well groomed
and sheds its needles with decorous elan
assuring us it has so many that it has life and time to spare.
Trees are bold but this one has been cut
and does not yet understand.
We water it daily to keep its hopes alive.
We await friends to share this evening with us.
We will light the fireplace and admire the tree
and sing songs if we can find the songbooks
or else chant them from memory.
We will poke our stockings in anticipation of tomorrow,
gently foot-nudge aside the boxes beneath the tree
in hopes of glimpsing our name on some of the wrappings.
We will thank our gods, our luck, our stars,
    our happenstance of time and place
and drink too much wine;
then of a sudden
we will again be alone.
We will bank the fire, unplug our tree
join in a hug
and climb the stairs that lead us into tomorrow.
Merry Christmas, Happy Chanukah no matter
    how you spell it,
Happy New Year.
Peace…

Screen

I am sifting for gold
and the sand is falling through.
Nuggets are not in my stars.
I am sifting for women
and my lines are falling through.
Lust is not in my future.
I am sifting for truth
and my thoughts are falling through.
Epiphany is not in my karma.
I am sifting for a poem
and my words are falling through.
Grace is not in my life.
Better to be the screen—it has function and does not know
    disappointment.

Universal Meaning
Through Poetry

Searching for understanding
of the me-ness of me
the you-ness of you
and if we could ever share common ground
in the we-ness of we
in a story that would bond the world together.

A poem of Mary's pain in birth of a God
moved the critic to find epiphany and revelation
in words I found mundane.
Unsure in my shallow depth of feeling
in search of common perception
marveling at disparity
depressed at division
disquieted by disappointment
I surrendered an effort at understanding
and nestled, relieved, in respite.

The solitary mind may not find peace
but may well find moments of repose.

Process of Erosion

I became self conscious
which is not a bad thing
as we should be aware of ourselves.
I became fearful
as I was not pleased with
the me-ness of me.
I changed my habit, habitats, haberdashery
and became self conscious of my new self.
I opted to be the real me—
but could not find him any more.

THE WEAVER

Somewhere
the harsh yet smoothed staccato
of angry buzzing
moves near.

I shut my eyes, imagining a benevolent bee unprovoked,
a furious wasp provoked by my very existence,
bullets shot from guns seeking my self,
or a playing card rippled by the bicycle spokes of a child.

Let the "it" come, and do that which each "it" does
in its turn, in its turn.
I am resolved to smile, to cry, to hurt, to die
in my season.

Random is the warp of existence,
time the counting strands.
My weave moves between unknowable interstices,
my life propelling me as my shuttle.

Fear is not the color dye I choose for the cloth of me.

WRONG ROAD

Northern lights inform my space
with flares of false color hiding causation and meaning
adrift in layers of air charged with unfelt waves.
I admire the evidence without understanding the crime.
On my road
dead ideas clutter passing lanes
compelling continuation to destinations not chosen.
The smell of skunk in the wind,
the thump of concrete seams on the tires of my vehicle
that is not there.
Life is a double solid line where
crossing may not be survived.

TOMORROWS

Hunted am I
in nights particularly
dark alleys and dank sewers of thought about
what yesterdays intimate about tomorrow.

Whispers of failures of what was done
and worse, what I did not do.
I declare accolades instead
in the light of self-deception.

In nights without sleep
I stare at the ceiling,
 rub my eyes hard to create starbursts
and demand the rise of dreams.

I sweat into sheets
drool into pillows
tremble for tomorrow
but leave the praying to you.

THE MISTAKE

I was in error today
and it was plain for all to see.
Now I am hiding
as a child would hide.
I am writing this poem,
ignoring the world.
I await the palliative of self-deception
when
I imagine
it will be ignored
it will be forgiven
it will be over-looked
so that it does not matter, as
the world is so disassembled into disfunction
that my error is not judged by my embarrassment but
rather
erased by its own patent self
and thus set aside as mere carelessness.
I do this to each of my errors, I confess:
I explain them, I excuse them, and then
I deny them palpability.
I control my world as if a page upon which I write in pencil
and I erase at will that page
and your very memory of it.
to remind me of this poem is an unkindness
and I trust beneath you.

ARMS AKIMBO

Arms akimbo
in a shadowed dawn
I face some future naked,
folds and flab no cushion
but neither an embarrassment
as we all are thus—
if we are lucky.
I stood here once before
fully clothed
to no avail
so decided to try with my real self on display.
I seek a hint before the answer arrives
alas, always too late to plan for it.

SONG OF THE MODERN MAN

I am headed home once more,
Not that I traveled far;
My heart left by my own back door
To find my distant star.
My family never knew I left.
Never knew I wasn't there.
Just that my heart became bereft
Of everything I had here.
My mind and soul took holiday
From my children and my wife.
Selfish thoughts held me in sway
And made me hate my life.

[chorus]
It's funny what folks do not know,
Their world hangs by a string,
But they can't know what you don't show
And—you don't show a thing.

I find that I am drifting back,
How long I cannot say.
Once you dip your soul in black
It's hard to find your way.
Each day was hard, each night worse,
You worked until you caved,
And your house felt like a curse
for the screaming and depraved.
One more problem, one more fight,
One more crying whine.
I may just hit that road one night
And not come back this time.
There's just so much a man can take
Of crying and of lying,
There's a point where you just break.
Road's much better than your dying.

[repeat chorus]

Safety First

They used an iron hasp of words
and a lock with only one key.
They set diversions on the path
and guardposts within sight of each other.
They slew the craftsmen who built the door
and burned the map to find it.
They melted the key and formed it
into a grave marker.
They thought that although they could not find me
neither could the others.
Thus I was safe,
and they smoked a cigarette and called it done.
If only they had remembered to put me inside.

THE SCHOLAR

I am locked in the yeshiva of my soul
midst guttural sounds and sentences that end like questions.
the language is familiar in cadence but undecipherable.
old people and childrens' corpses mutter to me
and it may be begging for salvation
and it may be merely a prayer.
corners are dark, the outside world excluded with purpose
the insides parsed, cut, turned, burned, exposed only to be
    re-draped in mystery.
if I cannot understand what you are saying
is it because I cannot understand what I am thinking?
who am I and
more importantly what am I—
better to be an elephant or an orca,
sentient but not intelligent enough to invent evil.
history assails me and I own it
distillate am I of all that came before
processed through taste-buds of forebears and my own pain.
when I go into the world from here I am ignorant of world's ways
and secure in my beliefs of god
not knowing that the former is a blessing
and the latter a curse…

Thoughts on Vacation

I.
Vacation is rebellion against what it is we do
when we do the things we do.
At first, a revel of freedom
then overtaken by fear it is ending only a few hours left
fear of returning home
a crushing sense of what awaits—
home never takes a vacation.

II.
A man gave me a cigar late that evening
and we watched each other's red tip
morph from fire to ash.
Cigar and vacation lost into smoke and darkness
as if neither ever was there.

III.
Bourbon Street on a Spring afternoon
crowded with teenagers
and people pretending to be teenagers
tourists carrying colored glasses of alcohol in the shape of genitalia
T-shirts with words never spoken at home
low belts freeing overhanging stomachs
flab jiggling to the music dumped from doorway
dusty pick-up trucks loudly following meandering people
with revved engines, radios rapping.
black men in torn jeans touting beads and voodoo readings
tequila and a taste of tawdry in the warm breeze

young girls in torn jeans touting themselves
future sin and a taste of tawdry in the warm breeze
black boys beating bottoms of upturned plastic pails
without even a place to drop down a dollar
but just for the noise.
Rumor has it the street becomes dangerous at night
later the worst
down side streets with little traffic, fewer eyes.
Hard to picture in the Spring noonday sun,
with Disney holding hands with Fellini and everyone pretend
and in costume.
The bars are dark counterpoint to the street
music live
singers whine in mock bayou
street signs inquire: ya want a slice with that Po-boy?
Drunk in spite of myself
drinking to spite myself
reliant on the rumor that bars don't put liquor in Hurricanes
but seems they do, to tell from the rising storm.

IV.
Passed out by seven
thirteen hours later
toilet for the ultimate piss
glance at the mirror and read my T-shirt wrong way backwards:
"Last night I got Bourbon-Faced on Shit Street."

Tales in Kelvin

Heat of sun does not burn
but rather punctures
just below the skin
enough to infect its wanderlust.

There was a time when I obeyed
what I was told
or suspected I had heard
by word or innuendo.

Today I am naked to the sky
dreaming of beaches and deserts
crabs and scorpions
my friends.

I will be wrapped in gauze
soaked in aloe
bathed in oils
tinged by warmth.

I do suspect
you have no sense
that although I dream
my core is ice…

Why so, you might inquire?
I shall not respond
for I am in fear
that you shall understand my answer.

SURVIVOR

I have survived this day
so far
perched as I am on the edge
—always on some edge—
of this rose petal.
The aroma has made me heady.
I have searched in vain for pistil anther stamen
to grasp so as not to fall.
This rose is so full of itself
a whorled funnel of flowers
a willful profusion of pretense
that it fails to help its most reliable of admirers.
The early dew chilled me
the day's evaporation floated me with rising vapors
and then radiance drove me deep into crimson labyrinths
where pollens filled my mouth and mind.
Now there is a swaying from breeze,
hint of evening summer showers
in the texture of air,
a threat of inundation.
Why do I stay, you might inquire?
The glory of shared sensations justifies my risk
like jumping into an ice-rimmed forest pool.
Tomorrow perhaps I will rest on the brown exposed bed
    of sunflowers,
or curl into a morning glory at dusk,
sharing a bed with bee and bugs
as great adventure invites strange company.
But
for now
 the edge of waxing moonlight illuminates me
enshrined in red temples,
a resurrection midst color of dried blood.

THE JEWISH JOKE

On the holiest night of the year
Yom Kippur
when the book of life is sealed
and, within, the fearsome list of
who shall live and who shall die,
the Rabbi, shaken by death,
preached his shaken faith
while decrying the common trope
that G-d was everywhere
and that all things were part of his plan.

The joke:

Two dead Jews arrive at heaven's gates
and await their entrance interview.
At one point they break out in laughter.
G-d, unused to such things, made inquiry:
"Wherefore dost thou jest over some event from life?"

"Oh," one dead man replied as if chatting with a friend over
    Passover wine,
"—you wouldn't understand—
you had to be there."

Comes now to the altar of truth
the most common of Jews,
that is every and all Jews,
spread across six millennia,
most years not for a blessing,
parsing the Jewish sentence of being chosen to serve
but living in reward the pains of Job,
the pillar of salt,

the barring of Moses,
the test Isaac,
the oils of Spain,
the expulsions and conversions and coercions
    of power and rectitude
the smoke up the chimneys
the pile of desecrated gravestones from an entire continent
    piled in a Paris cellar—
centuries that only can be explained by a shrug of the shoulders,
a sardonic joke self-inflicted in affirmation,
yes now thus comes your common Jew
be a him or her,
a rabbi or beggar,
a son of G-d or a son of a bitch,
not able to understand.

"They write scrolls and books about this,"
I could feel the rabbi say to himself.
Well, yes surely they do, but the answer
is hidden between their lines.

HOURGLASS

Pinching the hourglass by the neck
cannot stop the sands of time.
Where is the answer to the mystery
that freezes the sun below the horizon
and gives me another hour, or perhaps
an entire day?
I do not seek perfection but could use another chance
to find the words I failed to say,
the act I failed to perform,
the kindness that eluded me as I leaned forward into myself.
I search gods, sky and soul for the answer that can save me
as I effuse into eddies,
a cloud dancing among the winds.

The Nude Beach Revisited

on the littoral
sand eating my toes
	daring the waves
sounds of sucking
sounds of shell gravel
sounds of sinking lives
	wind counterpoint enter stage left
	gulls stage right, don't miss your mark
gods taking peeks when not obscured by kites
(you'd think gods could do better).

clothed in whole or part or not at all
but
	EVERYONE is stripped when you come right down to it
faces bloodied by their mind bleeds
spurts in tidal rhythm
nipples replaced by gills
and may I hold your hand
as my lust is palpable, naked
as I re-member....

Lachrymose

I am fond of the word "lachrymose"
although such is a melancholy attachment.
To have affinity to words is affectation
embedded in literary pretension;
I am guilty as self-accused.
But—
the word is expressive
useful in morose colloquy
(sufficiently abstruse for readers to grasp angrily
    for dictionaries)
and in sum wholly embracing my vision:
tears, the blood of our souls,
dripping down the meridians of a dying world.

Watch Out Below

A fragment slipped off the edifice of my mind
and shattered on the street below.
Stone shards, dust and bird feathers littered
the landscape of life.
To no avail
        no avail.

People are stepping over the debris of thoughts
        emotions
                broken burnt buried bits of pretension
and no one glancing up to see the source.

Sense of falling is not relieved by your pity
so keep it to yourself.

I am afloat in flotsam
ocean of false foam
waves rolling low on my shore.
The great breakers have always kept their distance.
I hear them from afar
tears of the gods roiling out of my reach.

Standing on a Rock

I stand on a rock
   my faith
breathing truths
   exhaling sin.

Winds assail my face
   presuming to drive me into darkness, but
my toes curl to anchor into stone
   honey rising in my veins.

Rocky tor commands view of all things:
   parched plains
   burning cities
   sinners abound.

My faith is gristle in the interstices of time
   sinews in my mighty arm
   bone of my rectitude.

You may fail
   sweat on your face a telltale of fear—
You shall fail
   you cannot follow me—
You have failed
   behold your mirror—

My body has been lately assailed by
   lice, flies, lies, life, and
I have bent to flick them all away but

when you bend your feet can slip, shifting for
    balance
    purchase
    purpose.

I can see you now, coming closer,
rot seared into your mind,
carried on winds of you, defeat manifest—
it is all on you, of course, and you cannot climb my rock.

Long night fills with epiphanies writ in stars
as prophets praise my faith
    my faith
    my faith
    my faith…

If now I stand on sand
the ground powder of my faith
grains blowing dispersed by winds
    whispers
    whimpers
    whines
ears filling with the weight of dirt
drums bursting
then there is pain in silence
forever forever.

May I blame you,
as you stood before me,
purveyor of falsehoods
slaughtering me in ritual surrender?

Beaten Day

the sounds I see
    float
    flaunt
    flit fly foam fume fill
myself with something I cannot understand.
if it were only ennui…
if it were only apprehension…
cutting onions
    acrid burn of eyes and throat remind me
    we cook and carve the carcass of our lives
and are left hungry still
    and burnt grit in the kettle of our soul.
stale metaphors assail me
    life is roadway
    life is process
    life is learning
    loving
    lying for the greater good.
this morning rose dank and angry on the horizon of possibilities
and phased downhill from there.

why is there no doorstop for the swinging hinge of time?
I had for a moment a sense of promise
    but then I opened my eyes
    and heard again the sound of the drum
there is a beat and pace drum drum drum
and there is hum humdrum humdrum
and there is all around me you us drumdrumdrumdrum
but just once I would like to smell the melody
override the basso drums
drums drums drums drums drums drum dru dr dddddddddddddd

Sisyphus prayed a favor be done him:
that the stone should grind him beneath as it
    rolled to predestined hell.

Sleep of the Righteous

The sleep of the righteous eludes me.
I am either not righteous or not being watched.
The gods are always everywhere so I must not be righteous.
How is one to know enough to adjust?
Am I redeemable?
If so, what is my path?
Am I forever spat out of grace,
a mere flick of tongue by my ultimate judge?
Is redemption only upon resurrection—
truth be told, I could use a good night of sleep while still alive.
Taught to neither complain nor beg, may I make
    so bold as to inquire?
And, how am I to know if I am being answered, and,
thus,
how to understand when no answer comes?
Hearing nothing, in search of guidance I must sleep on it
which, if you were listening from the start,
is the essence of my problem.
Those with insight
are asked to revert…
(if you are replying I am not righteous, please provide citations).

2

ABOUT MY WOMEN

Of course one never owns a woman, and surely I have never presumed. To the contrary, the reverse is likely true—women own men and may indeed so presume. What I own is the memory of women, and these poems are of that fabric.

THEATER

She played with words,
reciting lines she did not write,
feigning understanding,
guessing when passion was involved.

As a child she learned her cues
from faces and fears of others,
echoed them through life,
tropes of presumed perception.

Faced with uncertainty
of love or lust,
she could not recall the cues
nor recall the final scene.

So she lives her days
reprising answers to unasked questions until
when comes the curtain
she exits stage left in darkness.

THE SKIN OF A WOMAN
AT A RESORT IN 1983

I did not know her.
decades ago
in a pool
there was a dance or an exercise
(cannot remember which or where)
and we were to place our hands on the shoulders in front of us
and walk in a circle for a while.
the woman was young and plain
in the pleasant beauty of plain women
who understand that being plain is restful.
I remember her skin, dry touch
yielded layers of depth to my fingertips
shocking me with texture of fine-cut velvet
coated with sifted flour.
My pressure was so slight she must have presumed
I had another motive, although the motive was only the moment.
We walked for a short time, and then were asked to change places
and I felt her fingers on my shoulders
conveying revulsion and suspicion
as if she had devined my deep desire when touching her.
We next stood still, alone, closed our eyes and were told to think
although of what I do not recall, nor did it matter
for my thoughts were at the ends of my hands
and radiated embarrassed rushes everywhere.

When I opened my eyes she was gone,
There was no space where she had been.
Life folded over emptiness leaving only memory
of softness beyond skin
and revulsion for the person who knew her so well.

THE DIRGES

For some, as we know, April is the cruelest month. The below cycle was written in February, 2021, a month full of snow, cold, political unrest, pandemic uncertainty and personal malaise. The source of that malaise may indeed be attributable to the factors I have suggested above.
Or not.

chocolate ice cream

I licked chocolate from the corner of her mouth.
a favor done is money in the bank
when it comes to the doors of heaven.

she pretended not to notice
but I knew
she recognized the reason.

it was our only night together.
in the morning
the bed was empty.

the ice cream container held the melt.
I drank it, warm and thick
a rich memory that tasted like her skin.

when these days
evening is on its cusp
I look for her but

like the taste of ice cream
she has melted forever
into chilled interstices of my mind.

oranges

I smelled oranges in the air
that day
though far from any source.
air is a cruel tease
stirring non-existent memory.

these days
drifting
alert to clues
to unsolved mystery
her hair
and the chenille bedspread
of a bed never slept in

olives,
tarragon
sea salt from tears

alone

smoke in a bar
noise in the streets
music from somewhere
rain outside

thinking of church tomorrow
when God will explain
why when I cried no one came

aspirations

aspirations lost in a sea of yesterdays
my thoughts a syrup
poured on cold pancakes
congealed in brown eddies
failing of purpose
becoming markers of failed tomorrows

I watched hope retreat
down roads of analogy
metamorphosis
tropes
memes
unrhymed lines
seeking muses I never had

the man

nobody saw him on the corner
woolen cap pulled over ears
gray whisps escaping
pocked whiskey nose
hung belly
flushed spots on pallid flesh
right hand thrust into his bagged coat pocket
left hand raised in tremored salute

the wind called his name
but he did not hear

deep and dark

deep and dark
this life
stretched and skewed
across rambling night
ebony bird cawing
preying
praying
incantations
from far high cliffs
precipices fogged by premonition.

shattered like thrown crystal
in an empty fireplace
shards reflecting lost fires
of what we once called dreams.

we are all of us floating
on tides we do not understand.
beneath those silent subtle waves
we sink, buried with our tomorrows.

Regret

In her eye a liquid not quite tears
moistening pouches puffed beneath
when she recalled the last moment we held each other
in a time not yet arrived.
Thin lines edged her eye
a trace of teeth on her drawn lip
the tinge of gray woven in whispers of black
against the echoed tinkle of crystal dropped carelessly
    on that marble floor…

Marianne Paints Her Toenails Bright Green

(a love story)

Marianne paints her toenails bright green
which is a most un-natural sight.
Her feet are old, as she is old,
she wears laced up boots
so why she bothers I don't know.

Her toes curl downward
and on the tops are scraggled gray hairs.
Her little toes almost disappear beneath her soles
while her ragged nails punch holes in her support hose.

Legs are no better,
puffy purple veined and lumped
up to the cellulite above her knees
making valleys and creases on the way.

So those being Marianne's best preserved parts
I reckon I understand the green paint.
The scourge of Sunrise Highway she is,
known across Long Island
sweated and grizzled on beaches,
strolling the Miracle Mile in shorts,
a woman of a certain age
and a certain emptiness.

Marianne and her platinum Amex Card—
Yeah well, at least she picks up my tab…

SOMEONE

Someone sat up the night with me
winds through the cracks
bangs and shutters
held my hand
rubbed my neck
said it would all be good.
Problem being
someone never really knows
do they?
Comfort hidden in the shawl of darkness—
and next thing you know, sun comes up…

Careful Woman

She didn't have anything to lose
but still not much to say.
A closed and careful woman
who comes in your life one day
and when its done and time has come
she's already gone away.
My memory bears her perfumed skin
with music in my ears.
That's when my saddest thoughts begin
entangled with my fears.
So now I'm all adrift once more,
a condition I could cure,
but somehow I have chosen not,
I'm feeling all unsure.
I do not want to tell you more,
it just brings out my pain
of nights alone, sitting at home
with time to fail again.

Dismissal

I am no longer listening to you
hearing you
interested in interrupted interpolations
sticking things into my life where they do not belong.
You were intrusive which is
    to say
you touched my buttons one too many times.
You demand examples?!   That is so like you
the problem you have we have.
You foretold my acquiescence
    YOU WERE NOT MY TYPE (of anything)
You presumed to judge me
    PRESUMPTUOUS
You predicted the end of times
    TIME MARCHES ON
You anticipated wished crafted witch crafted my death
    WRONG AGAIN.
I have so much to
    see
    do
    dream and set then aside
    to waste my time
    marching to tomorrow over the detritus of todays.
There is a dawn outside which we may share
    when robins sing
    when cows come home
    when chickens come back from across the road to roost.

But you, sir, have work to do before you can share that moment
tongue flicking to reel in the flies…

Her Smile

Her smile spread across the sky,
knitting the brow of clouds.
Sun, sensing kindred warmth,
wove colored bands to highlight the land.
Below, perplexed, discussion
reflected confusions and doubts.

When her smile faded, its imprint,
godlike residue on a shroud,
lingered on the winds,
a reminder of what might have been.

SHE

She
puckish and unfortunate
crossed my meridian
beguiling and beguiled
with chips in her veneer
in unseen places.
I had no defenses, so needed not to lower them.
Snow embraced the ground outside,
while inside the heat melted judgment into desire.
The line was breached
Venus descended by infiltrations unseen
and barely felt,
until one morning
I awoke and she was gone.
Squinting through my window, all I saw
were receding footprints in the snow.

Dream Woman

invented a woman from my mind
porous, wet, warm
floating on desires that were mine
apertures
ideas   a bit of bone   hint of pi-i-i-ink
subjugated of course
why not, since you are dreaming
HARD STOP why is that?

a woman entered my mind
crags of dried clay
beached by desires not mine
closures
anger
pick a bone   splash of reddddddddd
going to be a problem
why not, when you are dreaming
HARD STOP get her out!

a woman made my mind
from bits of dried shit-clad clay
devoid of desires
zeroes
stone cold   dog bones sucked of marrow
bath of blackblackblack
not a problem
because I'm not dreaming
NO HARD STOP no stop at all…

Summer Beach

When you close your eyes, all summer beaches are the same.
Surf over gravel almost drowns out chatter and radios,
cries of children and gulls penetrate haze of mind,
smells of cocoa butter and peanut butter
mix with salt water in torpid air.
I remember when we lay so close your sweat
    ran down my arms and legs.
I remember when I rubbed oil on your back
    and you let my hand wander.
I remember when we slept shamelessly
    wrapped around each other.
I remember when your breath exhaled clams and garlic
    into my nostrils,
        so powerful that afternoon winds dared not intercede.
I remember feeling sand between our hips as
    we were together in the dune.
I remember being sure those days would never end,
so long ago,
when we were young and believed our world was also young.
If I could resurrect the lines you lightly traced in my tan arms!
If I could recall when our friction was warmer
    than sun-soaked sand!
If I could hold you once again without restraint,
find our smooth surfaces unmarred by valleys of time,
our tongues touching, meandering—
if you still loved me and if I could never forget…

Darkness has fallen on the beach.
I am warned of physical danger, lingering alone on the shore.
I am unafraid.
There is no danger as perilous as memory.

$\underline{3}$

ABOUT PAIN

Why such a depressing title? Because the subject itself is depressing this section must come here, as the following section is entitled "Death." But understand that Pain is not only a likely precursor of demise, but also a fundamental component of life. I didn't design that reality, so do not blame me; as my late father was wont to say when unhappy about something: "I'm not complaining, I'm only reporting."

Bleeding Out

In this potato salad morning fat and gummy
as, outside, icicles drip into the hearts of men
while inside untold hours
explode, excise, excoriate
against apocalypse backdrop:
what if the world failed
as in a grade C movie,
suggesting we build a fall-out shelter?
Rational presumption fails to provide survival,
after all?
When guys with flak jackets and AR 15s win
is there a question to be asked?
Or have we timed out?
Somewhere
        on the scaffold of time
    we are hung to bleed
    on assault ladders of life
    leaning on the ramparts of our future.

prolonged in poverty
seared is schism
abroad in anger
festering in fear—
all of which we celebrate today.
An olive branch I offer you,
to shed at last, at least,
your heathen fear.
Come unto us, you disguised and degenerated,
dark in skin and spirit,
quit your seething envy,
accept this love we offer
as manifestly we have proffered these many years,
an open gift which—
    —inexplicably—
you have 'til now failed to receive.

Heathen Envy—July 4, 2022

Yes, you prayed to the spirits of nature
might of mountains
ferocity of fox
docility of deer
claws of mighty cats,
a simple solution
for finding cause and meaning
placing no burden on ancestors
making no judgment as to failures
of those whom once you loved.
I can imagine, then,
the latent epiphany of our coming—
men of course but, yes, of clearly final knowledge
knowing the true power of our beings
universal in reach
patent in promise
of perfect rectitude
as only that which is true can be perfect.
This gift we bore but—alas
(and as is glibly said)
we cleave to beliefs embedded in time and life
for want of imagination
as we, this well known,
were made imperfect and in need of enlightened salvation
    and thus
—both our history and our today are indeed your fault,
a self-inflicted pain of ongoing duration
evidenced:
    overt in squalor of cities
    covert in dirt beneath Indian schools.

I AM AFRAID…

Looking out at snow
sweated armpits, eye sockets, toes
furnace pumping its dull rumbles
winds objecting at the shutters
glass rattling in its putty
cinders pushing through the screen driven by gusts.
The world on hold
waiting for resolution
perspiring in the face of Winter.
I am afraid.

WILLIES

Willy sat in his cell
wishing for more bars.
Stink of people
dead animals
hope denied.
The man across the aisle eats an apple,
his leg dangling off the top bunk,
chomping as his eyes blink in sequence.
Eating is not allowed in jail cells
but no one is in jail.
Of small moment as no one has an apple,
but William cannot tell.
He is left only with that pun as punishment.

Another Sunny Winter Day
Boston, MA

Sun bright and everywhere
floods out of sharp air blue sky and cold
onto the skin of the world
matted with the snowness of white.
I squint
as who does not
before the revelatory demands of clarity for today:
the kid's blood in the alley, knife on the ground
the old lady full of virus dead in her room with no one to care
the woman in his car trunk/ don't piss off the guy/ too late isn't it
and go down to Dot Ave and see them lined up
call them of color but they know they're something else
going to wipe down the toilets of empty offices
with pictures on the walls of kids
sitting in front of computers in Beverly Farms
costing more than they earn in a week.
Sun snow sin sinking at dusk
all balled up and blended
like it doesn't count to untie the strands
like the threads are blooded already
and to look at the truth, well
who gives a shit
I ask you.

DIE-COTOMY

so many righteous

evil times

prayers offered

fervent rhymes

the just forgiven

dark holds sway

God-given pardons

read your paper today?

understandings

not understood

promises

do no good

ascendent

decadent age

love

hate and rage

[color race, religion sex, gender, history, their their-ness]

[   ]

love, we say!

then explain today…

FIRES/MARCH 2022

I piled the wood carefully over paper and kindling,
cross-hatched and balanced, with proper space between logs,
made sure the flue was open,
gently touched the edge of my match at bottom
watched dark smoke and burning shards of newsprint
    flutter upwards
then catch of the wood and sudden flash of yellow flames
lightened smoke
push of warmth behind the fire screen.
Outside through the window, cold winds stirred the snows.
Staring into flames while kneeling before the hearth
felt like praying while the world was on fire.

I read newspapers and watched television carefully over coffee,
processed and assessed with balance and space,
made sure my mind was open,
gently explored the reasons and reactions at bottom
watched dark smoke and burning shards of cities flutter upwards
then catch of the wood and sudden flash of yellow flames
darkened smoke
no push of warmth behind the television.
Outside, through the screen, cold winds stir the snows.
Staring into flaming images while seated before the news report
feels like praying in my pew while the world is on fire.

Far above my house and far above Kyiv
pollution defiles the sky…

NIHILIST

He believed in nothing
other than his own existence
with each day a black mark in the closed ledger of time.
Searching his mirror for his better self
he failed to find a reflection, but
common as he was to all of mankind,
he was not surprised.

Love given him was passing fancy, and
his reciprocation a reflex of social comity.
When family and friends seemed to care about him,
this only heightened his suspicions.
If each day was its own reward, nonetheless and surely
it must cost him a day at the end of things.
Death of a friend he processed
as a personal warning.

He often wondered what life was about;
he simply wanted to wander;
while strolling around, it all petered out
in streams of desultory squander.

As nihilists have little to say,
this is the end of this poem.

HERE COMES THE MAN

so when the man comes down on you
not a lot to say but
swing back
fists wrapped in words and promises
iron left in mine shafts of weak resolve
on the road outward from the core.
I did not reckon on sunny days
ever
so when they came they gave me anger
an interruption in dealing with life.
somewhere the man beefed up on steaks and guns
and outflanked the defense I built
which proved to be air.
last person to prevail is the one whose knee-caps were replaced
with cyborg parts
all the nerve endings disconnected.
you coming with me
or is fear the end of your line?
bring the A-1 Sauce if you're a player
and get the fuck out of my way if you're not.

4

About Death

I am disquieted by the number of poems about death; while writing, each stands alone and does not appear as depression or preoccupation. I have edited out a few, and reclassified a couple under more benign headings, yet so many remain. I cannot say that it is fear, nor does it feel like anticipation, that leaves us with the twenty-one pieces which follow. To fail to read these poems means you will thus avoid the troublesome topic of death but, notwithstanding, that does not mean that death will avoid the troublesome topic of you.

Ashes to Ashes

There is dust in the air.
It sifts though sunlight as subtle specks.
It falls on leaves in gritty grains.
It sneaks past window screens,
not content to stay outside.

Dust and I, we are not friends.
I blink it from my eyes,
wipe it off my kitchen table,
gather it in shaken mops,
sneeze it back into the world.

"Ashes to ashes, dust to dust."
So they say.
How do they know?
Dust does not declare its provenance
nor speculate on its destiny.

What is constant in our lives?
Air, water,
days of sun.
Nights of moonlight,
food and sleep and memory.

Dust surely is too small, too petty
to be noticed on so grand a list.
It is an annoyance,
an afterthought,
like politics, or love.

If I became your dust,
during my lifetime or, likely, upon my death,
and were then to enter your body borne by wind,
will you taste, then, my uniqueness?
How am I to know?

TY @ THE HALL

Tyrus Raymond Cobb.
Tyrus Raymond Cobb.
Who were you and who are you now?
I dream some nights of old Ty Cobb
wanting to price his absolution from error
and justice for the lies they tell about him.
People dying with regularity from causes
    regular and irregular—
the dead, they are just like us
but not like you
Tyrus Raymond Cobb
Ty Cobb!
Ty Cobb!
In a good year I bat 250 at life
and do not spike the second baseman
(though I have often thought I would enjoy it).
I never stole a thing, let alone home fifty-four times.
I never beat my son so what's it like, I wonder?
Is that a lie, also?
I am running my bases, base and baseless
no foul lines to guide me
and I let it slide,
let it slide.
Slide, Tyrus, slide.
Your plaque says you were voted to heaven with four dissents
preferring hell and take 367 with you.
Who knows the voodoo that you do so well
digging dirt down the third base line, dead as a nail now
slide, Tyrus, slide.

HE DIED LAST NIGHT

Someone I know died last night
leaving people I know saddened
and me confused.
Easy to walk away with sense of mortality
or dearth of immortality
more likely.
Easy to compare age, health, family history,
pallor of skin at last meeting
to give birth to defense against fear.
Easy to note that
we all gotta go sometime
as if that is an answer.
Easy to break into tears
and then feel
that you paid your dues.

When I went to bed the first thing in my mind
was whether I would wake up today
and it was the last thing in my mind
when I couldn't fall asleep last night.
We mark death as personal: how much does it hurt me
or how much does it guilt me
or how much does it analogize to me
and how much time must I stay mournful
or appear mournful
and what does it mean to mourn when there is nothing
    to do about it.

At least when I die
I will not have these problems.
A solace of sorts…

April 13, 2022: Items

1. I have spent the last week sending condolences to people whose dear ones have died from sundry causes at untimely times.

To each I have dutifully emailed my condolences, freed of the tyranny and pricing of Hallmark.

To each I have said "May your loved one's memory be for a blessing."

To each I have suggested that their personal task is to live, and to "remember tomorrow" today.

In each such missive I have hidden my own confusion, fear, distaste for the sun's audacity, mocking the day of regret with the light of promise.

2. A friend of mine, returned from Poland, is going back once he arranges a supply of drones. The Times runs constant pictures of dead people and children. Today, the back of a toddler on which a mother has written a name and birth date, in case the parents die and the child survives their escape.

3. I have stopped wishing people a Happy Holiday although both Easter and Passover approach; they reply that they will not have a happy time because of a recent death, crushing both of us.

I have stopped looking forward to each day, a violation of my own admonition that we must embrace the future.

Each future has the gestalt of the past.

4. We are returned from a wedding in New Orleans, a port
   city like so many with much dull desolation punctuated by
   pockets of money.

Bourbon Street, so famous I could not resist, a tinge of danger
amidst music and alcohol pouring out of doorways. I follow a
small parade of horns and clowns down the street. Who doesn't
love a parade?

I awoke 13 hours later holding a large bottle of Tequila I purchased
on my way back to the hotel.

Flying home, looking out the window, I wrote poetry on the
airplane. Somewhere over the nondescript landscape of a
nondescript State somewhere between Bourbon Street and
Boston, I wrote this:

It is Spring.
There is no snow.
Vegetable America blooming beneath me
Trees hearing our roar
Children looking up at the place of the sound
Not knowing that sound is memory and we have passed
    far onward in the sky.
They perceive as today what is simply history,
and think they are looking at life…

THE KNIFE

There is so much common wisdom about life and death,
sardonic asides, dark aphorisms.
Proof it is something on the mind.
Sometimes…

"All you need is your health."

Life exists on the sharp edge of an infinitely sharp knife,
a balancing act that takes no prisoners.
Slip off and you are gone
step down too hard and you are cleft in twain.

"Life sucks and then you die."

You are not issued a balancing beam
sweat obscures your view
the knife is curved and serrated
and someone has taken your shoes.

"Life is what happens while you're making plans."

My knife is whetted by blood, honed by fear,
rusted by tears,
angered by experience
informed by a desire to jump.

"Here today, gone tomorrow."

I am dancing on the edge of my knife
as you on yours.
Stay sharp—
ah, a poor admonition…

"Live as if you expected to live a hundred years, but might die
to-morrow."   —Ann Lee

My knife is whispering about tomorrow
but it is a tease.
It is beginning to wriggle beneath me.
It is causing other knives to kill the ones I love.

"We never live; we are always in the expectation of living."
                                                       —Voltaire

You!
I'm talking to you!
Keep your goddamned hands off
the handle of my knife…

[as published in Ibbetson Street magazine]

Too Soon

Too soon too soon
it is always too soon.

Loading shells in the den
plaid shirt and face hair

Flat on his back looking up at the Pleiades
ground light from the barn down the hill

Too soon too soon
it is always too soon.

Cigarette ash dangling
Yingling in hand

Graveled voice calling
Almost country drawl

Too soon too soon
it is always too soon.

Stand back from the line
live ammo here

A pat on the back
and a smile for the kids.

Too soon too soon
it is always too soon.

Sad dog in the roadway
glad dog in the pick-up

Carving a turkey
turning the burgers

Too soon too soon
it is always too soon.

A brother a brother
and sometimes a bother

But always our brother
our brother our brother

We and God know it is too soon to miss him
too soon to miss him, it is oh so too soon.

[*For Stephen U.*]

LES FLEURS DE LA MORT

prologue
A lesson in French is in order.
This poem is not about love.
At least, not the kind
that you had in mind…
You perhaps read "L'amour,"
a romance of the heart.
But in la langue francaise,
"la mort" is "death."

a poem about the flowers of death:
And so they began to arrive
promptly
beautifully
in non-somber profusion
in splashes of red and yellow and orange and gold
in pots and boxes and vases
with little tags about watering and sunlight,
as if our family death had rung a bell in some global florist
to rally our true and dear friends to stop
    *

    *

    *

 and wonder how we feel
and decide, with beauty in their hearts,
that colorful symbols of life and hope and Spring and cheer
would, well, not quite divert us
(that would be unkind presumption)
but rather would at least console us
as tears fell like bouquets, in profusion;
then sobs would come in spasms
then sadness would fix its vise on our visage

then resignation would reign in our souls—
and we would be left with so many wonderful flowers
telling us that we are not alone
that life goes onward
that there is color and wonder in the future
and, as the last dying petals drift onto our floor
we might scoop them up
place them in a crystal vase on our mantle
placed next to the urn heavy with the dust of death
to echo the yin and yang of human existence,
finding peace.
I look at them now
arrayed in our room that gets the afternoon sun,
perched on windowsills
atop the piano
on the tables
perfuming the air
perfuming our vision
still fresh in bloom
(they have lasted several days, they must have been expensive—
thank you, kind and generous neighbors…).

I look forward to falling petals
markers of time
that, rumor suggests, can heal
the unhealable tear in the fabric of life and memory
where the gap spreads so wide that no bridge can be imagined
and where we do and do not crave resolution
as resolution moves us forward but brings guilt
    that we have forgotten.

la fin
For whom do we cry when someone dies,
I have always wondered.
For the dead? they have either nothingness or heaven,
    so tears are unneeded.
For ourselves? tears solve nothing and their flow
    thus unheeded.
For humankind? it is our lot in life—well, in death, I guess.
For the god who made death? not a question I dare press.
I stand midst les fleur de la mort,
perplexed in every dimension,
cheeks barely dry and eyes reddened,
waiting for the petals to fall, at last, at last
to usher out the past…

Poem Without an Adequate Title

Someone dies and you cry for those who loved them.
Someone dies and you tremble for yourself.
What is the feeling of death
the feeling of after death
the last thought
the last fear
the last rasping breath?

Blessed are the blessed who believe
in something.
For those who are unsure there is hope.
For those who are sure in disbelief
what is there? Such is the birthplace of
faith.

For the young, death is grief,
a tear in the fabric of certainty,
a moving of the lighthouse and you still at sea.

For the old, death is a
darkening mirror.

All rally to their calling:

the young know they should carry on as their future is long
and there is time to ponder—later.

the old carry on—
short time to fulfill their childhood promise
to ponder: faith or only fate…

SURVIVOR

We die by age
we die by ailment
we die by war
we die by accident
we die by conflagration
we die by indifference
we die by plague
we die by gods or Gods
we die for revenge
we die for neglect
we die for anger
we die for politics
we die for religion
we die from religion
we die for others who died
we die for ourselves.

We remember for pain
we remember for power
we remember for forgiveness
we remember to gloat
we remember to relish it is not we
we remember to cry
we remember to bask in our kindness given
we remember to forlorn our kindness withheld
we remember in guilt
we remember in fear
we remember because we cannot forget
we remember because we are seers of death.

We hold ceremonies for the dead
while we are alive
which is, all things considered,
consistent with what we believe we ought to do
as we exhale sighs of relief.

And may his/her/our/their memory be for a blessing
although who grants that blessing is not answering
and rumored not present.

Amen...

BECKY

She smelled of cinnamon
and the puffs of flour carried in the creases of her blouse.
Her gait was slow, her walk was stooped from
bending over the wooden table,
kneading the dough early each morning.
When she worked the counter she barely could reach over it.
Most-times, she preferred the kitchen, breathing the hot dried air.

Raisin bread
   croissants
      cakes with frosted peaks and small flowers
cookies in layers
   and with nuts
      and sprinkled crystal sugars
napoleons with many layers of jam.
She stirred the bubbling kettle of chocolate and
   often dipped in her finger
and licked it off.

As a child I would come to the bakery and there she would be
later I would come to the bakery and there she would be
I came with my daughter and there she would be
I came with my grandson and there she would be
—suddenly she was old, but I missed seeing the steps.

Becky had those watery blue eyes that make people nervous.
Her hair was held tight by netting
her entire life; I imagined
she slept with a net pulling at her roots when she shifted on her
pillow.

The day after she died, my grandson came back to the house
    with a bag of coconut cookies
And I told myself, I said:
"Let that be a lesson to you"
Although I was not sure what was to be learned.
Some people are there your whole life and then they are gone.
You are not so much sad as annoyed.
I did not cry.
I ate the cookies.
And then I said to myself:
"Why these are the best cookies I have eaten since I was a child."

Valentine's Day

the sun bounces up from the sheen of snow
but makes no progress against the biting chill.
trees are still, absent wind there is silence.
distant low rumble of the furnace
promises the house will be warm
and form frozen icicles like boned fingers
directing, from the eaves, untaken ways to hell.

light skews through shutters
a pattern moving across indifferent walls
marking time in sufficient detail
for what we have in mind.
being in mind is important today
important bulwark against the cold
leaking from here into a dying world.

we are sensitive to such things as time and light
snow and cold
warmth and respite.
death is immune to all of it;
death is the force we would will ourselves to be:
eternal, nocturnal, diurnal, ephemeral
force and power that lives forever in itself.

today and far away from here
where the sun rises from the sand
and informs the tumescent day
death has visited in its silent efficiency
to no end
but an end nonetheless
and we are left to ponder detritus.

oh to be death ourselves
without emotion time light dark
just finality of force
immune to fear
essence of fate
walking snow and sand
free to be ourselves.

what are the pronouns,
the descriptors of death
that we may properly address it
as the spirit compels us?
"me me" and "all of me"
"us us" and "all of us"—
lay us down in sand or snow and leave us be.

tears freeze on cheeks—
best to stay inside.
tears wet the dry air of the room—
to no avail.
the future compels and we should obey
as it is the best thing to do—yes?
other benefits of being death—no tears, and you understand
tomorrow.

[*for Eleanore*]

THIN MINTS

Life is thin mints
sweet with unexpected heart
but gone too soon
and delivered in such a small box.

My plate of thin mints was set out for a party
but someone kept turning off the music.
Ever try to dance
when the music stops?

A Speculation on the Nature of Touch and Time

Can you feel a touch through time?
I ask because I need to know.
When we are dead
or are apart
or otherwise indisposed
and memory fades into wherever stale dreams hide,
when evenings turn cold, alone and themselves prone to fading,
when hearts would beat if they still held a reason,
when hours and years and centuries erode the fabric
    of who we were,
when returning to your favorite beach finds only stones,
the sand carried afar by uncaring tides to places you
    cannot know—
will I still feel your breath when we sleep,
your hand find mine when we stroll,
your fingers on my aching neck in the darkness we call night?

APOLOGIES TO SPINOZA

Sitting in the springtime sun
thinking about looking for god.
Is it a person or a thing
single or multiple
tangible or ephemeral?
Understandable
(or if not, elusive on purpose or
by reason of failure on my part)?
Is he she it benign, evil or
tabula rosa on which to write myself and thus
by definition
etch the measure of my need?

Does death matter to my inquiry—
whether I live or die, does that prove or disprove anything?
Some have promised me life forever by reason of god
others aver there is no forever and thus no god.
But each assertion may be true or false either with or
     without a god…

I am told by my youngest son
who knows such things
that ancient gods were conceived in familial context
riven by contention with parents or siblings
anthropomorphic echoes of kings in power
to prove kings held divine right,
a pretension that trickled down time
as a convenience—but not to me.
I am also told that gods are inscrutable or I am stupid—
indeed I am told so many things by so many
yet not one such message bears the clear signature of god.

Beauty stirs from the color and grace of a flower
brought from garden to dark house and then again
    brought to the sun
to hear its message. But what I hear
comes from within me, a ventriloquist of beauty
and perhaps a skill given me unwittingly (to me)
by the god I seek. Is god
the net perception of my own proteins and electrons?

I hear from a neighboring house squeals of children
over something joyous or
at least
not sensed as harmful; yet,
life teaches me that among them
some will kill for profit
some will kill for sport
some will kill by negligence
some will kill for country
some will kill for vengeance
all will lie for all of such excuses.

And some will lie, steal, kill
for love hate convenience
bestowing pain and tears on those most loving of them
by word
by deed
by rejection
by abandonment
by death.

Of what truth has any god informed me as I face these children
and my mirror?

Has god ordained, predisposed, left to chance, resolved
    in judgment, or
does god not care
as these things are not god's department.
Perhaps gods do not have a job description that
    includes bottom lines.

So many have scaled the cliffs of souls:
prophets, rabbis, priests, philosophers,
my favorite mountain climbers Spinoza and St Thomas
the young on some cusp
the aged on some precipice
the wise and the stupid
the chaste and the venal—
for would any god
or man
dare deny one's thoughts of god and self?
I am told (I am so always being told) that
the silence of gods is meant to turn us inward to learn truth
but nonetheless I am unable to find understanding within.
I am told (I am so weary of being told) that
I cannot gain the wisdom to recognize any merit in what
    I choose by whim.

The flower rests on my table overlooking the garden
the sun a constant intrusion into mind and winter cold
perspiration creeps its way down creases of skin to burn my eyes
and I am again a child
blindly leaning on a lamppost at dusk
on an austere street in the middle of the city
as all my friends scurry to hide
leaving no telltale sight or sound
as I whirl with purpose
and scream into the darkening sky
"90, 95, 100, ready or not
HERE I COME."

RED BICYCLE

I have one request for how I am disposed of once deceased.
I do not care if by fire or earth.
I do not care if I ascend or descend.
I do not care if I am feted when fated.
Nor who attends if anyone gathers for any purpose.
I assume when I am gone I am totally gone—
except for the going rate for my bones and body chemicals—
as no sane person would seek body parts from such
    a worn-out enterprise.
However—
and here I hesitate to admit inconsistency
but
I would prefer to be buried with my Schwinn.

In 1953 I was riding my Schwinn Black Panther bicycle
up a hill in Brooklyn, New York locally known as Dead Man's Hill
for reasons rumored to relate to the Jewish Mafia
(whose existence was also rumored to be rumor)
when I was unceremoniously dismounted, dismembered
    and de-biked
by a gang of hoodlums who,
I learned upon awakening in Kings County Hospital,
had stolen my new Schwinn Black Panther bicycle,
then state of the art
with an electric horn built into the cross-bar between
    seat and stem.
In later life, fortune has brought me the solvency
that results in middle-class souls owning bikes of great promise—
super-gears
racing tires
drop handle bars
promising speeds well beyond the vigor of their owners, but

don't we ever look cool enough to take the Tour de France
    by storm,
our yellow jersey taut across our robust chests.
This last weekend
on Olde Cape Codd
riding my racing bike on the trail towards Ptown
clicking gears on a deluxe derailleur (selected by a son expert
    in such things),
and being passed, in my decrepitude, by men, women
    and children of all ages,
seated as they were on super-bikes just like mine,
I recalled the time when I rode my Schwinn Black Panther
    through the Borough of Brooklyn
sure that all eyes were upon me, awed by my power and grace.

Call me sentimental,
I am serious,
I assure you I am sentient,
I ask one last thing of you.
If you put me in the ground buy a wide casket.
If you turn me to ash find a wide oven.
If you throw me into the sea at high tide then accompany me,
in all cases, with a Schwinn Black Panther,
color red, seat black,
working horn in its compartment.

Please make sure that the horn batteries are fresh—
you never know when you might want to signal.

Leavings

What do you leave
when you leave?
—a husk
—a shell
—an idea in the wind?
If nothing remains
does that mean there was no purpose to you?
If the world ends leaving no one to remember you
does that mean you never were here?
If all you have for comfort is the thought in this poem
of deepest fears and inevitable truth
does that mean the answer does not matter?
Is it that the questions are best not asked, or
that they are best not answered?

Let's Talk to the Dead

dead she was
will stay.
moving on moving on.
people come to gawk but recoil
gray flesh too much a future mirror.
I am in that other space place dimension convention
and we are chatting:
    1. how's the air down there
    2. do you miss us yet
    3. are your nipples hard

alive she was
didn't stay.
moving on moving on.
people didn't see but recoil
life too much a reality mirror.
I am never in another place space dimension convention
but we are not chatting:
    1.
    2.
    3. button your shoe

What's the matter – you're not chatting—
chat got your tongue?

Bury 'em deep 'cause
rumor has it
they smell almost as bad dead as alive.

Timber

Floorboards in my old house are cut the wrong way
with the grain, no doubt how the millhands were instructed.
Straight lines from wall to wall tell no story,
inviting empty walks, otiose moments.

Wind felled the elm, doomed soon by whatever random pox
    has doomed all elms,
and my man took to cut and stack the trunk for winter fires
up against the porch
in the lee of the eaves.

A few cuts from low on the trunk
were set aside,
in need of splicing,
too thick to yield easily to cross-cut teeth,
and on these huge cuts could be seen the rings of summer drought
of spring rain, of early autumn,
a diary of elm-hood
and of the land.

Counting tree rings is no small task—
do not believe them when they tell you differently.
Rings are not perfect, and confuse.
Rings meander in echo of tree shape.
Rings are many and keeping track difficult.

One day I rolled out the largest cut into the sun
and with fine sandpaper evened out the nicks and digs
the uncaring saw had left on the face of time.
With the tip of my pen I counted from inside outward
and at each ten rings made a gentle mark.

When the crust of bark was reached, the last winter's storm
the death knell,
I heard you speak to me:
"Your great grandfather planted me today and I had a joyous year
with sun and rain and supple winds;
your grandfather here worried over me, with so many years
of cruel dryness in the skies;
your father here hung your swing today, your fourth birthday
and here is where you fell from your swing,
you can feel the bump in your thumb which did not correctly heal.
In the midst of lush summers your daughter sat here beneath me
reading first Goodnight Moon and
later
Catcher in the Rye.
Three rings ago, here you buried your wife,
the marker seen through my low boughs on the crest of the hill.

When you pass, your children,
gone to the city all,
will sell this farm
and men will come to dig out my roots
and then I too will die, as you,
into eternal eternity devoid of time and space and history.
My lowest rings will be ground to powder and float in the wind.
But I shall not ring in that moment
for dead is gone for man and elm,
as for all things you and I have seen…

Tell Me No Lies

He held his cards close to himself
because he knew what should be done.
He froze his face to mask emotion,
quell expectation,
disguise strategy.
At casino, at his club, even at friendly games at home
he was sure of his opacity. There was
no way in hell
he had a tell.

He ascribed his constant losses to bad luck,
or that the stakes were so low that no one correctly assessed risk,
or that the law of averages would average him out
over time. Yes,
time would tell.

He lived his life close to his vest,
the consummate professional in business,
the storybook husband and father,
eschewing emotion in favor of constancy and leadership,
creating predictable expectation,
devoid of hint at manipulative strategy.

When she left, he had hopes for a next wife.
When his children avoided him, he blamed a past wife.
He carefully calculated his path,
marshalled life's chips,
stacked them in neat colored piles
as he felt them wither between his fingers.

While engaged in dying,
he had one thought alone, as he had no time for another:
did his entire life have a tell and, if not, then
he needed more time to average up.

*A tell in poker is a change in a player's behavior or demeanor that is
claimed by some to give clues to that player's assessment of their hand.*

Harvest

I serve my country
on fields of battle
so when you see me coming
I do enjoy being thanked
for my service.

My service is of a special sort,
as I am tasked to save my brothers
whose wounds may leave them
alone and in harm's way
and in mortal peril.

My method is perhaps of interest
and indeed my commander
has begun to inquire
as to why all I bring back at great risk
are dead.

I share with you my special rules
as I shop for blood on fields of war:
I retrieve only those already gone.
Their families deserve to know of their sacrifice.
Their bodies are for a blessing.

Seventy-Nine*

Each year there is my birthday poem
looking backwards, looking ahead.
Backwards is filled with nascent trends becoming waves,
everyone is dying.

Depressions marked my year,
not an auspicious omen for my future.

Let's chat about death, shall we?
Are you pro or con?
Does it turn on who is involved?
Do you quote Woody Allen to be okay with death
so long as he isn't present?
Is death of another your trigger to ask
"What does this mean for me?"

When you cry about death
do you cry for the decedent
or for survivors who must live with it?
or for yourself
owning your own fear?

I paused today to plan what I will do when I die.
You are not able to think about your not existing
and you exist in your mind,
not in the flesh-box that carries it around.
Will I be asleep? Dream? Forever?
blessed by avoiding the 3am visit to the toilet?

Is it possible to understand "nothing"?
If you live in thought, what happens when your brain
is burned
eaten by worms
becomes proverbial dust?
No wonder we are declared to have a default position
of having a soul, which
however improbable,
is easier to understand than the alternative.

I admire insects,
not so smart they say, yet
when you try to step on them
crush them in a tissue
swat them with a rolled magazine
they run like hell to stay alive,
avoiding the "nothing" that even they understand
    they cannot understand.

Some believe gods created men
for some reason;
some believe that man created gods
for obvious reason:
it is easier to think of some something ephemeral
than to think about nothing.

I am damned today
    to be without proof of options
    to lack data
    to read literature of no use
    to contemplate my 79th year filled with
        bodies in caskets clutching beads
        surrounded by flowers
        faces frozen in refusal to answer my questions
        watching dark powders pouring from vases into rivers
        and oceans.

I am seventy-nine years old today.
Happy birthday to me…

By the time you read this, I will have turned 80 years old. Feels a lot like 79. When I have something more to say about my age, I will place it in my next book. Stay tuned…

5

About Everything Else

When you categorize everything, are you surprised that there is stuff left over? Some things are just their own stuff. Section 5 contains that stuff.

New House Across the Way

Across my street they are building a house of presumption.
My neighbor sold his house to a builder who tore it down.
I do not blame my neighbor; I never cared for him
but he is gone so blame does not matter.
I cannot blame the builder because tearing things down
is a thing that builders do.
And he is now building a house of presumption,
presuming that some person or family would choose
to buy such an over-conceived contraption as this new house,
opposite my modest structure of honest colonial charm.
Will not a buyer look outward and declare me out of scale
and not grand enough to have guests stare at from
    out his broad windows?
Or will the buyer look only inward
reveling in the scale and accoutrements of his own self-image
and expect his guests to do the same?
Will the buyer enjoy the noblesse oblige of deigning
    to permit my presence
in his purview, as lords of old smiled as the serfs shuffled past?
Will the buyer use this new castle only on occasion,
    traveling continually
to the "continent" or the "orient"
or to the casino in Deauville?
Will the buyer have children
and will he allow them to play with mine,
perhaps first verbally qualifying my son by casual,
    revealing inquiry?

When my wife brings them a bottle of wine
and a fresh-baked loaf
in neighborly welcome,
will the buyer graciously invite us in to imbibe and chat,
or will the buyer provide a stiff thank-you,
close the door,
look at the label on the bottle
and pass it to his cook for the beef bourguignon?

I think we shall snub this buyer when he finally appears,
as he is too problematical even today,
before there is grass on the front yard,
before the labels are scrubbed off the new windowpanes,
before the scaffold to set the roof tiles has been removed,
before this troublesome buyer
(I can picture him even now)
saunters within view,
his imperious gaze demeaning our existence.

Next thing you know, he will be demanding half my crops
and droit du seigneur upon my daughter's nuptials.
What a cad!

Kemel and Edie

Kemel Attaturk and Edith Piaf were seen holding hands
Madison up near the galleries
singing a song my mother sang to me
from the thirties, or perhaps before:
"I gave you up just before you threw me down."
His, an unexpected alto counterpoint,
hers with the smoke of cafés in her rasping whine
while at a dark table in the rear
Josephine Baker hummed along
all the way from Paris
just before the fall when Bogart made the train.
The names remind me I am not at fault,
no guilt to share,
only a melancholy I cannot understand.

Tequila*

There is a song with that title
and everyone knows it
but the only word sung is
"tequila."

That makes sense because
after all
what the hell IS it
and how do they get the cactus needles out of the bottle?
Why does it go down so smooth
and mess with you in the morning?

Tequila with a beer chaser!
Tequila with a cigar chaser when everyone went home
with the wrong coats and too much tequila.

I woke up to a Tequila Sunrise this morning
and my woman was not there—again.
"Took another shot of courage"
but tequila in the morning is not recommended—trust me.

You may not find this poem very poetic but, then,
who's to say?
Not you, you're likely hung over.
But not as badly as me…

*There are simply not enough songs about tequila but here is a riff on two of them.

AHOOEY AHOOEY*

Gauze strips of evening
replaced by shrouds of night
seem seamless progressions
hiding omens of fertilized evil.
Night is a many-car train
drawn by an ancient coal engine
with dark caboose, endings not revealed.
Intervening cars carry people somnambulant
tankers full of vitriol
hoppers full of diggings from unknown lands
and box-cars—
many box-cars—
their sliding doors shut tight
concealing cancerous cargos.
We are, each night,
hoboes by the track
clustered around fires
shedding scant warmth and light,
no insight to where that night will bring us.

Odd we do not rebel against the sunset
shred the gathering gauze
demand accounting from darkness to learn
what awaits at the end of the line.
But…

I understand reticence
acceptance of denouements
when placidity promises possibility of peace.

We are shoveling coals into the fire box,
ignoring sting of sweat in our eyes
aches in unwilling arms
welcoming repeating clack of wheels
seduced by train whistles stretching across our darkness.

The plaint of Ella Fitgerald mourning blues in the night...

[As published in Ibbetson Street magazine]

Dolores' Ice Allegory*

there is frigidity in the air today
dripping to the ground
congealing into ice
hiding my fields
cracking my tree limbs
the sharp splintering sound muffled in soaking air.
in boots still it is dangerous to walk
you may fall, at your age not best
or simply slip-slidin' away.

where are we bound this January day?
looking for love
lust
forgiveness
or just an excuse?
do we all live in fear, Dolores?

if we had a destination we are promised to lose ground
or at least never arrive
like the line on the graph approaching ever closer to zero
an infinity of lost opportunity
notwithstanding fervent effort
fervent desire…
in the song, God makes his plan
but seems it is not a shared vision
it is a mystery
as it must be lest it be found in error
an unforgiveable sin for an omnipotent godhead.
Lack of symmetry favors me
as no sin I commit is unforgiveable even if unforgiven.

I am out on the ice,
feet bare,
if I do not slip-slide then my soles stick to the ice in painful grasp
if I do slip-slide my soul sticks in the sleet
cold and unrequited.

I have kissed my boys without explanation
and then turned around.
I wonder if they know for sure
or only suspect.

I earned my chill
sought cold steel of air and water
begged to be flogged
begged
sensing it is fair recompense for what I am.

who am I
I cannot say.
but I know one thing:
I'm slip-sliding away.

This last of three poems based on songs will strike no chord with those not Paul Simon fans, but next to Bob Dylan and Harry Chapin he is my favorite musical story teller—well also Giuseppe Verdi I guess…

Lives to Live

Some of us are born and die and that's it.
others return in various guises animate or inanimate
or so they say.
Some of us claim to be reborn in our own skins
a metaphorical event, rapture aside.
Some of us claim immortality
but change of address, taking the elevator upwards
or downwards;
it depends.
I have no quarrel with any person claiming entry in any cohort.
Life is hard enough without standing in the way of its resurgence.

I do have a memory of myself being born
that comes to me as in a grainy black-and-white newsreel
blood and shock and everyone screaming—
but only once.
Perhaps this is just my first time around
and much remains in store.
Perhaps repeated lives are parceled out only to certain elites
and I did not qualify.
Perhaps I held the golden ticket
but by ill temperament or fundamental error I received
neither chocolate bars nor salvation.
I am curious but do not know where to inquire.

My father claimed immortality every day he awoke
taking each sunrise offered as a gift to be used,
although to him the highest and best use was leisure.
He was of Edwardian birth, and never captured
the disease of being American.

My view is to be resigned,
as being without a vote in the matter.

Rambling Heart

Ethyl Mertz and Ed Norton
get chatty with Noam Chomsky
about the meaning of words as indicia of worth:
is content more important
than constancy of character?
If we know what someone will say
before they do so
are we comforted,
as safe from the confusion of surprise?
Peripatetic proclivities produce provocative permutations
while Chomsky is unusually sullen and devoid of opinion.

We are admonished
the modern canon
to write poetry bare and terse,
seeking boiled-down essence of feeling and thought
swift delivery of reduced essence
intense gravy from the meat of life.
Where does this leave the rambling heart?

DISCONNECT

blue sky crisp air
cold
winter
sun gives everything sharp delineation.
the eye sees precision
predicts
understands.
the mind deconstructs,
images bleed to margins of perception
and fade in washed pastel colors.
Monday things should be clear
at least for a while,
the week has yet to do its evil, but
seems it's not to be that easy.
is this a matter of fault and, if so,
who or what to blame.
we can accuse disease,
age of the observer,
last night's wine.
all lead to remorse but perhaps
it is more a time to recognize a greater clarity:
sharp lines are illusions
leading to false action.
true knowledge may lurk at the fuzzy edges,
where simple answers are revealed by sunlight
as too simple.
the world is a subtle fabric.
to assert understanding robs you a vision
of the reasons you always fail.

LEVITATION

I rose as a flower at dawn,
unfolded to receive promises
was kissed by rain and breeze
coaxed by afternoon sun
and did not see the nighttime coming.

FALL

Well what do you mean by that?
The season?
The devil's descent from heaven?
Did you just trip on the stair?
Do you perceive you have fallen from original grace?

Where are you now—

dragging through an unpleasant place?
I would relish hearing the details.

Surrounded by falling leaves crisp underfoot?
Not interested…

Sulfurous fumes embracing you?
Wake up, you're dreaming.

But the feeling is reeling, casts a pall?
Revel then in the stench of your fall.

You are found now among human-kind
and hence a stench of a different kind.

You sought redemption?
Not on offer in this store.
You sought kindness?
Not for sale on this floor.

You want to check redemption's cost?
You're seeking something forever lost.
You'd settle then simply for peace?
That's not redemption, just release…
You now retreat to wanting love?
That's not granted from above.
Love comes at random with a meter to feed,
but feed you must to sate its greed.
You earned a pass for rectitude?
Insincerity leads you to self-delude.

You claim enough erudition to know
what sages and kings learned long ago:
you only reap that which you sow.
Honi soi qui mal y pense.

Would schadenfreude assuage your pain?
to compare only diverts your brain.
Was comfort denied while your back was turned?
Repetez mon ami: what have you learned?

Hall in Fall

rain on the street
sheen over black
dull sky and street lights reflect off the skin of the world.
trees drip randomly
cold dollops
trickle down hairlines and bounce off lashes and cheeks.
Fall is falling
falling hard
falling uninvited on the unburied corpse of Summer.
birds and squirrels
understand, scurry
as I am standing with shivers and mouth agape in disarray.
How did I spend sunshine?
I don't recall—
too casual to treasure it, too lazy to remember.
some are depressed
by gray as world motif
but I cannot complain as no doubt all my fault through inattention.
My hallway
is carpeted with wet leaves
as my shoes drop their cargo, dour evidence of
    death of living things.

Failure of Flowers

Tourmaline sky
whisked clean by autumn wind.
We stand among our shadows
moving sun aslant
as we bury her in still-warm ground.

Why do my perennials bloom only now?
They were needed in austere Spring
more so in heat of Summer.
They failed me then, mock me now.
Do they know?

WAITING WINTER/WARMING WORLD

Out my window, silent stone walls divide New England into
    squares of loneliness.
I see rain, wind, hail in November,
trees holding red bloom in a warming world
as our turkey steams on our Thanksgiving table.

Leaves flow like waves over yards and fields,
stick together in mattes of muted color,
wedge into soles of shoes,
deposit a trail of evidence on kitchen floors.

Where are the six turkeys who strut down my street?
Where is the coyote who ate my neighbor's dog?
Where are the white-tails who left my lawn littered
    with rabbit scat?
Where is the family of deer spotted round the corner
    one recent evening?

There was a bear eating trash the other day,
famous now with his mugshot first page in our town newspaper.
Birds are no longer twerping me awake each morning.
I am awaiting winter's arrival, seeking its excuse for
    its unseemly delay.

Snow and Analog

cold white curtain
gauze with light and form behind
coats my grass
bends my trees deeply.
I hear the snap of broken boughs
the skid and crash of cars
the slip of my neighbor, an old man who should know better
than to be abroad in a storm,
playing over intermittent whoosh of winds.
snow is like love:
gentle to admire,
rising above the undertones,
dangerous when embraced,
casually brutal when it falls.

WATER

he was all about the water
   bursting
   crying
   nursing
   drinking
   sweating
   shivering in snow
   evaporating
   trickling like a river
   drowning in salt seas
   washing up on unknown shores.
now he is wet sand between your toes.

Boxing Day

Inherited truth slithered down my memory,
masking
seducing:

Mother thinned the catsup before she poured it on the noodles.
Back from marching, spittle wiped off my cheek
and
from the floor above
the drip of water and
someone crying.

SKEIN*

Mired in muddy water
we aspire to join a skein
to soar in communion with our kith and kin
symmetrical formations of power and grace
so that, looking up,
others will exhale the long low breath of admiration
rejoice in our purpose
and smile at their own good fortune to catch sight of us.
Although better to do so with birds of other feathers,
nature does not yet have that much joy on offer,
and humankind has yet to embrace those possible heights.

* *"A group of geese is properly called a gaggle, but only when they're on the ground. In the air they are a skein."*
>   *—The Little Book of Answers, pg 124*

ROBIN

Didja ever notice that robins hop
but not for me?
Burning feathers mark my way,
offerings of my offer.
Didja ever notice that suns set red in the summer
but not for me?
Night is made for black suns
hung in my sky.
Didja ever notice that all creatures are made in her image
but not for me?
Warped men follow me from ahead
cluttering my time.

Too much to put on the bird?
Tough—never did me wrong but no matter.
You will find hard candy in your stocking
stuck to the walls of fabric, presucked by life
    and covered with fine robin's breast hair.
You will find your own feathered nights and warped men
and try to blame the bird but
    truth be told
this one, YOU own.

BREATHING

Do not breathe deeply
as there is water in the air.
It will pool in your shallows
darken below your eyes
blacken your armpits
float your eyeballs
wobble your tendons
soften your knees
jelly your spine
and drown your mind.
Wait then for the dry winds from the forest,
cleaned by pines and oaks, cedars and willows,
white air bouncing off peeling birch,
blue-clear in day and black-pure at night,
and only then breathe deeply.

Morning

Hungry morning
imagining feasts and pleasures.
Comfortable noontime
sunned by possibility.
Tensed darkness
hints failure in the air.
Blindness of night
is precursor of the false promise
again
of dawn…

Good Morning

Hard particles from tears
collect in the corners of your eyes.
Gently you coax them outward,
avoiding pain and false stars in your gaze.
The grits on your skin have hard edges
and are whisked away with care.
It is a daily ritual,
done without judgment.

Next morning, before you repeat
what may be error,
think what role these sands of sleep fulfill.
They carry the seeds left by your dreams
and perhaps are better planted than discarded.

Bonfire

sticks and twigs and dried leaves that burning blow

and branches now green and crackling

today's paper

this evening's left-overs

the restraint we had

the hopes we lost

the goals we missed

and the smoke is burning my eyes…

Tossed Salads

I learned last Sunday
from the strangest place,
the Times crossword,
a phrase I never knew,
"word salad."
I dismissed briefly its legitimacy until
that very day
I came across its unashamed use in another publication.
I am ecstatic as I am a salad man, yes indeed,
prone to rejoicing in my salad days.

Into each day salad I will toss the morning and the stars,
breezes and the aromas,
flowers and the birds
blue my favorite color.

Into each dinner salad I will toss lettuce of three kinds,
blue cheese with veins,
oil of olives
tomatoes shaped like torpedos of deepest red.

Into each word salad I will toss long words
emotive words of crying and laughing,
objective words that meanings refine
by words that rhyme at the end of a line.

THE ALLIGATORS ARE COMING

The alligators are coming, I have been informed,
teeth overhanging jaw in implicit menace.
I must revert to study crocodiles as perhaps there is confusion.
Here in the snow I would think them slow and ill-adapted;
regardless of species, the March sun will not stir their blood
and the melt will not permit immersion.
Same is true of the people I know,
being human and ever malicious,
disguised until prey succumbs to confusion.
Inherently slow and ill-adapted to evil,
the March sun stirs not my blood but only my memory.
We are prey to all manner of risk, real to be sure
but the only imagined is more dangerous,
it corrodes perception, inhibits judgment, destroys trust
and thus opens us to all things that would do us harm,
weak and ill-adapted as we are to live with each other.
The Everglades hosts the tail-splashing lurches of greenness
that may give us the startle we need to retreat.
Here in the city we do not enjoy such warning
that follows each shake of our hand.

The Newlyweds Kissed

The newlyweds kissed in fading sunlight
while everyone stood and applauded.

The newlyweds held hands, swinging between them
as they skittered down the aisle.

The newlyweds waved their free hands
acknowledging the ocean of smiles.

The newlyweds danced under overhanging boughs
while a thousand candles lit their night.

The newlyweds laughed hearing prepared toasts
with gentle and humorous jibes.

The newlyweds sat with friends at afterparty
as older guests drifted down the darkness.

The newlyweds hosted a farewell breakfast
with hugs, clasped hands, coffee and promises.

The newlyweds then brushed their teeth, rushed their breakfasts,
rushed to work, cursed their cursors and shopped for laundry
detergent and a pre-roasted chicken on the way home.

There is no magic in the air once the guests are departed;
twinkling glints rest only in the eye of memory.

Baboons

Once upon a time
in Jo-berg
long ago in a languorous summer
we were warned about the baboons
who force themselves into houses
by sending babies through small window cracks
and then improbably opening doors to the troop.
Once inside they become vicious
punching and biting
throwing bottles and feces,
to be extracted only by backing away
until they have had their fill and leave
with devastation in their wake.
We saw these baboons in the hills at dusk
seemingly benign
far away and engaged in their own lives,
found invasion unlikely and thus,
over time, lowered our guard
and were fortunate not to pay the price,
although neighbors were not so fortunate.

Marvin

Soft diaphanous pale
misunderstood by many and himself
hopeless
one day in New York was given a flyer for a bar where people
    were not what they seemed.

Simple syrup is just sugar in water
but simplicity was denied
through no fault he perceived his own.

His life worn like fog off a cold ocean,
observable in a bar where Marvin is not what he seemed.

Burning Egos

shirred egos
dessicated /decategorized
sizzling in oil
could burn your tongue.
gods, governments
families, fears
shimmy in the pan.
"what's shakin'?"
wrong question.
live in your pan
be your pan
cast iron for caste lives
lived in heat.
can't see over the rim
no visibility except continuous wall of iron
odor of burnt
sweating retinas
at sea in aqua
cannot swim
ears hear the taste not the sizzle.
tingling in my toes.
"who owns this fucking stove?"
ask my mother
she's dead but knows everything, just
ask her.
I'll set the table
we'll eat the food
you'll drop the dish
which, an artificial concept,
leaves no shards,
but there are splatters of ego on the floor.
looks like shirred egg.
never knew the difference one letter can do…

The History Café at the Sixth Ring*

Garibaldi was overheard
the other day
sharing with Bismark how hard it was
to build a nation.
"Not so," said Alexander, who
was lighting his pipe
using federal greenbacks:
"Just give it a try and two centuries later
they will be literally singing your praises."
"Parvenu!" spat Plato, an aside to no one,
his usual audience.
The chorus of masked former Presidents
chanted a refrain about how the US of A
built many nations
by burning them and resurrecting them
free and devoid of corruption.
Everybody refrained from sniggering
as ring six was dependent on foreign aid.

"Politics is poetry on the ground,
rhyming people in rhythm with beauty!"
"A wonderful thought," said Golda Meir,
clutching her mother's large purse
(a dollar fifteen at Espenhain's in Milwaukee).
"Who said that, anyway?"
From a lower ring a voice wafted upon heated air:
"Well, I did—but not for your ears!" hissed Adolph.

An awkward pause… but then
conversation resumed, as it always does
in the History Café at Ring Six.
"yadda yadda yadda yaddy diddly hi ho hayah—"
so saith one and all.

*The sixth ring of hell houses heretics doomed to eternity in
flaming tombs.*

Winners

Gray autumn rain is a weight of feeling
laid sloppily on slick leaves and crunched acorns,
ridden by unpleasant winds into alleys of blowing platitudes,
hidden by gloaming nightfall,
rats chewing scraps in the corners, ignoring damp fur.
Lean in, they say; the latest catchy advice of the wise
    to the willing.
Lean into your mission, your purpose, your goal, your life.
Do not shirk your imperative,
finesse your promise,
bury your future in among ineptitudes and fears.
Are you not inspired when you do not say "cannot,"
energized by the sun-promised tomorrow?
Well, then, open your front door
stride into that street
absorb those cold pricks of spray
allow your hair to escape your hat
soak your shivering ears and shoulders
lean deeply into autumn gray
resist its weight
embrace its promise hidden
    somewhere
        in there
and take no guff from the bullying wind. But…

Down the alley rats are laughing
their bellies full—
they look eagerly as you lean too far,
hearing your nose break and your eyes blacken
as you pitch forward to the pavement.

"Leaned too far, didja?
Tough shit, kid. Ya know—
eatin's pretty good down the alley.
Ain't much headwind, either."

CAPE COD IN THE WIND AND RAIN

Talons clutched on top of a reed,
bending in rhythm with the wind,
red wing blazes dulled by thin cold mist
sent by ambivalent gods,
obscuring clarity in sprays of disinformation.
Gusts blow towards Armageddon but the talons at first hold,
stalwart against destruction,
not Megiddo but upon this spit of land stuck into desultory seas.
What can you tell of a flat plain, or indeed of Zion on high,
far from dank marsh and sodden sands,
on a Cape crowned by armies at sea in search of food,
    not salvation?
Gusts arise, descend from no direction—omen of random
    comings,
second or third who can know,
so many claimants in the interstices of time.
There is no history for the red-winged bird
oscillating in unknown winds,
but only the clutching now in a drizzling fog
where hawks abound and christs sing Armageddon's mantra
to bending air, ruffling feathers in foreboding dusk.
Taking flight, prophecy becomes proof
and across the marsh the sound of hawk wings
is softened by the dripping blood of kings.

[as published in Ibbotsen Street magazine]

Hard Cider on My Mind

Idea(l) of woman:
rock candy sweet
inside the hard crust
cymbals symbols clash clatter
and the noise and the rocks never melt.

I waited for flesh
but got something more, an idea
of what flesh would be like if it did not smell
when rotting.
I lacked proper bait
the tide washed the marsh clean of what I needed
sulfur filled the wind and stung my eyes.

I love the promise of the idea
but somehow it does not reprieve my expectations.
Like mushrooms sprung suddenly in Spring showers
I am filling
with rain that is not quite water, but contrived.
Colors bespeak poison.
I cannot swallow, from judgment or fear.

It is a shame,
hard cider being on my mind
and lacking time and a glass…

Gods Hang Out

On the corner of my street
on the way to the store
out of beer
wouldn't you know it but
there they are
just the ones I am trying to avoid—
God themselves.
"Howdy," they allow in casual familiarity;
they really know they make me nervous,
how to get under my skin,
tweak my guilt,
tempt my residual modicum of fear.
"Hey yerself," I allow with downward glance,
stepping off the curb
as you don't want to crowd them
(I learned that a very long time ago).

"What's your hurry," they ask
all friendly like—that's part of their trick,
they want you to remember you once were real close friends.
"Goin' to the store," I confess, glancing aside as I am
    walking in the gutter.
"Oh, beer run. It'll wait, ya know; hang a bit, let's talk."
I really don't like talking with them.
"Ain't got much to say," over my shoulder, I am almost past.
"Then listen to us," and you know when that call comes
you owe it to yourself to pay attention;
who needs the risk of ignoring them?

"You are our son and daughter,
our glory and yet,
to see you,
perhaps our own original sin.
You are upon our mission even today,
the bottle you buy will hold distillate of our sunshine,
microbes of our own conception,
craft of the hand of your brethren.
You breathe our air
into lungs of our devise
as we offer you today
transitory peace, in which to craft your moments.
Thus
we are with you
entire
even now."

I stop and turn
but there is only one last message in the air:
"Ya have a nice day, ya hear…"

Q

I had never written a poem title beginning with "Q."
A discovery in reviewing my poetry list
from 1970 to April of 2020.
I found this odd and,
of the view that prompts can come from anywhere
I set out forthwith to write a poem that could be catalogued
under the letter "Q"
which mean nothing tendentious nor abstruse
as the undertaking itself took the texture of a game,
an amuse,
an exercise in humorous mode.

I must confess I had qualms about the task,
as it seemed contrived and unworthy.
How to weave a piece of quality from such
simple yarn?
What quixotic whim could make of this conceit
a thing worth reading?
In anticipation, my mind quivering,
I sat before my humble computer and—
wouldn't you know it, in the quiet of my room
the words came to me, one after another
as in a queue, quite a flood, I could not quell them
and I knew my quest had been fulfilled.

(Dedicated to Webster's National Dictionary, desk version, published July, 1988, pages 604-616)

THE NIGHT WE EARN

what to make of day?
born as they all are with promise
harbinger of dawn pale yellow-gray morphing into blue
in light resplendent…
have you read the news today
or seen its eclipsed pathos on your screen
or spoken to a friend ill with unknown symptoms
of unimaginable import?
the child kidnapped and found slain?
the rebels stealing girls into servitude from their schoolrooms?
the wild and crazed gunman wreaking random chaos?
the taste of dry fire on the wind?
counterpoint waves sloshing streets?
soldiers securing cities midst starving families in flight?
the sun, appalled, beats retreat with nary a drum to mark its time
and night, ashamed it has been assigned at random to this day,
shrouds the evidence of whom we are in guilty darkness.
some learn not to rouse themselves at dawn
these wise and wizened witnesses who see the world
   in the mirror of their eyes.
and those who wander forth in wonderous light:
should they not know better, these inheritors of
looming night that shrouds but does not forgive?
at the first touch of dawn, then, draw your shades
close your newspaper
let your phone and your computer go unanswered
for you were alive all yesterdays
and so you understand today roiling in the streets
repeating incantations
begging for the dark.
if you presume to have a soul, best bury it, for
souls are fragile constructs
not built for life among animals such as we.

Sore[n] Losers:
Ode to Kierkegaard

One: Hang yourself and you will regret it

"Do not hang yourself and you will also regret it,"
we are advised.
You might think this a defeatist life view
or an invitation to sloth
or to evil without consequence.
I think not.

There are times you will win
and times you will lose
and times when you will not be sure.
(You may not be sure when you die…)
If you do not play,
where are you?
Did you bring your own dice?
Did you shave the cards?
That's the point, it does not matter.
You did not design the game.
The thrill comes once you ante.

Two: But now it is finished

"and I never want to see her again,"
declaimed the seducer.
You might find this the cynical cad in gloat,
or an effort to brag to the barroom.
Those conclusions speak only to the mind of the hearer
and not of the speaker.

Driven by external reviews of one's life,
this may be ritual response, check the box.
Driven by internal demons,
this may be expiation.
This may be confession of error
or false sense of sensibility, as if
anticipating the clear intent of the victim.
Are you victor or victim?
Are you always one or the other?
Who is keeping score?

Three: Fear and Trembling

Is it what you feel when God tests you,
high on the mountain with the sword above your son?
Or is it how you feel today,
or every day?

Bibles are transmutations
so what can we make of this phrase?
It is surely thematic;
we receive God with it, we think of God with it
and we are coaxed to find our salvation with it;
pick your chapter and verse.
Is your fear a test—and of what?
Who was there, to ask Isaac?
Well, God but he's not telling.
Isaac is said to be fearful he had not understood.
Was death violative of moral law?

Christ did not ask us to follow moral law.
Christ asked us to love.
Is murder an act of love?
Is piety love in your heart?
And if you hold it there,
is there a need to show it?

Four: Dialectics

Explains the universe
to all for us.
Soren seems not to agree.
Things do not move with history
and we are not part of history.
You are yourself regardless of context.
Teleology takes away the freedom to decide
for the world decides for you, and negates
making a difference.
Must we retreat inside to find ourselves
regardless of time and place?
They create books about this.
And religions.
If peace is a choice of either/or,
what is it a choice between?

Five: The meaning of life

Only four steps and here we are,
the answer to the question you came to ask.
Life is understood only by history
and lived only tomorrow.
Are you your own work in progress and,
if so,
can history help?
Are we to be driven inside by anxiety,
by powerlessness,
by what people say of us when they measure us,
and what do we owe them,
those with their scales arranged in front of our bodies,
our acts
our failures that are not failures?

Six: Says Soren

"Whatever one generation learns from another,
no generation learns the genuinely human
from a previous one."

Chateau Parvenu Goes to Dinner

We are drinking the wine of sunshine and rain
squeezed strained barreled nurtured
as if warm breezes and gentle drizzles can be transmuted
into tasty sugar and alcohol after being stashed in dusty fruit
for months on end, pecked and filched by sharp bills
dodging frosts typhoons twisters drought mites
random lightning jags,
finding its way to bottle label truck
shelf with an incomprehensible description below
($39.95 and so well priced)
tasting as pine needles on the forest floor
stones in a stream
spices not found within a continent of its birth
leather and coffee and pitted fruits
wood of all sorts old and new
kept for years on its side
guarded from heat
salted with droplets of cork
viewed with candlelight
poured into decanter
repoured into glass, whereupon
journey completed

it is assigned a number purporting to describe its merit
or lack thereof
as if a high school student submitting a purloined essay
	for extra credit
while drinkers, taste deadened by scotch and coffee martinis,
drop into it ice cubes, water, seltzer,
wines of different provenance
spilling it on surfaces
leaving gummy lip residue on it margins
sloshing it for smell
viewing it for color and streaks on the inside of the glass
combining sweets and tarts
red depth with fair fish
gold clarity with larded roasts
and the dregs stolen by teenagers
then drunk, excessive lees and all, on the porch while inside
old men pontificating over cigars.

American Litanies

They came looking for us, unaware of Eric the Red
deSoto and da Gama
Raleigh and Hudson
Drake and de Leon
Magellan and Verrazzano
Champlain, Cabrillo, Cartier, Cabot and Coronado
clueless Columbus
his statues now defaced with red paint,
    broken noses on the ground
seeking those who trudged the land bridge looking for a home.

Now they speak
    French in the South
    Inuit in the North
    Spanish, Chinese, Creole, Italian, German
            and everything else in the cities—
but only "American" on the Plains.

They grow
    fruits in the West
    grains in the Middle
    liberals in the East
    data sets on the coasts
    microbes in the labs
    hate everywhere.

They claim to be
    democrats, demagogues, demi-gods
    republicans, replicants
    pedants, pedophiles
    professors, professers
    atheists galore:

Jews
Christians
Muslims
Buddhists, Confucians, Zens, who can keep track
all confused, confounded, co-opted and conned.

They devour what they produce by
    labor and lust
    genius and greed
    power and perversion
    hubris and history.

They slay their victims, and all are victims
    kids and killers
    tots and tyrants
    students and scholars
    sinners and sinned against
    marchers and misogynists
    whores and holies
    white, black, brown, yellow, mulatto, tan, bronze
    a palette of death.

And the killers are given
    a skate
    an escape
    an injection
    the gas
    a book contract
    a white pointy hood with a militia T-shirt
    an AK-47 with inscribed golden stock
    to boast on the dark web.

They sing of
    starred banners
    spacious skies
    Abraham and Jesus
    death and destruction
    race and riot
    peace and prosperity
    rhythm and rap
    blues and bitterness
    usually out of tune, often alone.

They write
    tracts and tirades
    poems and porn
    screeds and sophistries seething with
    wrath and resurrection
    flowers and fears
    love and hate
    revenge and revelation
    revival and retrenchment
    todays, tomorrows and, most often, imagined yesterdays.

They are
    shot or sick
    shot and sick
    vaxxed or vexed
    deniers dying
    home-bound or hell-bent
    young and uncaring
    old and cowering
    black and suspicious
    democrats demanding
    republicans rebelling
    plane passengers punching
    sick and tired and tired of sickness
    seeking to regain their normal
    not knowing that in the history of this world
    what is normal is today.

They are this poet, this reader, this listener
in this moment and space
all sighing and saying it is for good or for ill
all knowing it is for a curse or a blessing
depending on where you have been placed by unseen hands.

THE WILL—AN AMERICAN HISTORY

Below is the text of
A WILL FROM THE YEAR 1745,
purchased in an antique shop on Cape Cod
several years ago.
Following is a poem written about the
(imagined) life and death of the illiterate testator.

In the name of God amen. The tenth day of June, 1745

I Nathanell House* of Yarmouth in the County of Barnstable
and Province Of the Massachusetts Bay In New England Yeoman,
being of Perfect Memory & Remembrance, Praised be God do
make and ordain this my Last Will and Testament in Manner
and Form following viz----

First I bequeath my soul into the hand of almighty God my
maker, hoping through the meritorious death and passion
of Jesus Christ my only Saviour & Redeemer to receive free
pardon and forgiveness of all my sins; and as for my body to
be buried in Christian burial at the direction of my executors
hereafter nominated----

Imprimes I give and bequeath to my dearly beloved wife Esther
House the great room of my dwelling ?????????? naturall life
and the privilege of the one half orchard by my will is that my
two sons Nathaniel House and Zacheus House whom I make
and ordain my sole executors; that they shall pay out yearly to
my said wife Esther House sixteen bushell of grain, to pay ten
bushell of good Indian corn & four bushell of rye and two bushell
of wheat yearly during her naturall life and keep my said wife
a good cow sumer and winter during her life and find my wife
sufficient firewood during her life and to provide and keep her a
good hogg well fatted for her yearly during her life. Item. I give

unto my well beloved daughter Hannah Seares fifteen pounds
in the old tenner** to be paid to her out of my moveable estate.
Item. I give unto my daughter Rebecca Hall fifteen pounds in
the old tenner to be paid to her out of my moveable estate. Item.
I give unto my daughter Esther House eighty pounds in the old
tenner to be paid to her out of my moveable estate and my will
is that my daughter Esther House shall have the privilege of
my Great Chamber for as long as she lives ????? and cut ?????
firewood as necessary for her to live of off my wood lotts as
long as she lives unmarried. Item. I gave unto my Grand Son
Nathanell Sears one new Bible. Item. I give unto my Grand
Son Nathanell Hall one new Bible. Item. I gave unto my two
sons Nathanell House and Zacheus House all of my lands
and meddows and cedar swamps and buildings except what I
have disposed of already in this within written will with all my
moveable estate to be divided equally between my two sons
Nathanell House and Zacheus House to them and their heirs
and asignes for ever on condition that they pay all my just debts
and legacies as my executors to this my last will and testament.
Revoking all other wills and testaments.

For witness where of I have hear unto set my hand.

his

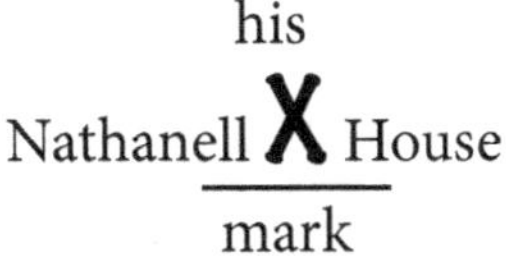
Nathanell X House
mark

In presants of us

his

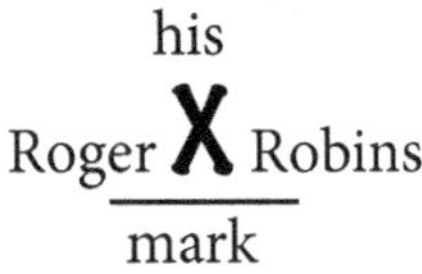
Roger X Robins
mark

Joseph House 3d [signature]
Joseph Slaple (sp?) [signature]

** It is likely the family name was, or came to be, "Howes" and not House, based on genealogical records much later gathered. The original calligraphy appears to be a poor rendition of "House" and I have chosen to leave that name in honor of my initial enthusiasm for my discovery of Mr. "House's" will.*

***Originally I had assumed this was an archaic spelling of the word "tender." According to my son Charles' research, it is a reference to the "old" English ten pound monetary unit (distinguished from the more current Colonial version). It may be that in fact our current usage ("tender") is in fact derived in the same fashion, but I leave the pursuit of that detail to others; it has been hard enough to get this far.*

Apparent mis-spellings appear in the original. I do not know if those spellings were correct for the time, or if the scribe was in error.

ABOUT THE WILL

The will of Nathanell House of Yarmouth in the Province of the Massachusetts Bay in New England, a yeoman so self-declared, grants his daughters sums of money, and leaves his dwelling, meadows, cedar swamps and buildings and remaining assets to his two sons, provided they grant to his wife a life estate in the Great Room of his dwelling, and annually "bushells" of grain, good Indian corn, rye, wheat, a good cow, firewood and a "good hogg well fatted." A man of seeming means, he signs his will with "his mark,"—illiterate. His soul is given to Jesus in expectation of a pardon of all sins. His body is given to his executors.

A Poem About the Will

I.
I am a yeoman of perfect memory, praised be God
and I leave my estates to my dearly beloved wife Esther
and my five children in rightful proportion,
as such proportion is judged this tenth day of June of 1745, and so:
my daughters are given money of the old tender,
    much more to the one unmarried,
and my wife receives from my sons an annual supply of
    food and lumber
and the use of the Great Room of my dwelling
and all else of course to my sons who are men
and bibles to my two grandsons, lest they not forget who they are
and who made them.
I leave no record of granddaughters for they are beneath
    my beneficence
and no doubt will marry stalwart yeoman all.
my bibles given are to be new; I am godly and own a bible but
it eludes mention and disposition;
perhaps it is so clearly the purview of my dearly beloved wife
that to even mention it is unneeded and perhaps unwise.
would that I could write to inscribe in its pages the name
    of my sons and grandsons…

II.
I miss today, nearing heaven,
standing in my "meddows"
reaping rye and wheat from the fields
sloshing my cedar swamps
harvesting firewood from my "wood lotts"
for I am a farmer indeed, proud
although I can neither read nor write. No matter
for I am of the land and of my God,

blessed with heirs and daughters
and many men to tend my lands
—what more can be asked of my only savior and redeemer?
I need make no mention of the stirrings of men
and talk of war.
Cape Codd and my family are blessed today,
my sun shines this glorious day when I praise my God
admire my estates
enfeoff my sons
provide for my wife
yes—proud in my province
my lawyer cataloging my wealth and moveable estates
as I inscribe my X mark in bold flourish
as befits a yeoman and a Christian.

III.
Did he die in the Revolution
did his sons and grandsons
the husbands of his daughters
his grandsons in a different war?
does the Great Room still stand
and appear on tours by the Historical Society of Olde Yarmouth?
if I were to roam graveyards would I find their stones?
if I were to roam graveyards would I find their memories?
even of Nathanell testator, he of "Perfect Memory and
    Remembrance"?
do his children's children's grand-children walk the
    summer streets of Yarmouth
sail small skiffs in the harbor
crunch their teeth into sugar cones stuffed with melting
    ice cream from the shoppe
look through sun-proofed glass at yellowed drawings
    of the ancestral home,

even perchance dwell in that dwelling, walking the worn boards
    of the Great Room
reading the family history in the old bible, notations in
    the hand of Esther the younger
or Esther the older although not likely—
are we allowed to hope and dream
even if all are dead
erased by war and plague and time
diluted by the seed and memory of others
a stain on the ambition of Nathanell
a loss of hubris echoing two and a half centuries
murmuring in the wood lotts
sloshing in the cedar swamps
swaying in the wild rye remaining in the meddow
without pedigree or memory?
Would Nathanell wish to return
if I asked permission of He of "Meritorious Death and Passion"
to create a miracle so that yeoman true
might learn if his stolid anticipation of forever has been fulfilled
or
is that risk too great, to ask both a presumption and unkind?
is his body best left in the ground of Christian burial
and his soul at the right hand?
perhaps we who make wills to ordain the future
are blessed, most times,
to be absent when the future weaves the world
    from shards of history…

*(Next time I am on the Cape of Codd I shall stop in Yarmouth and
armed with map and Waze seek out the old Christian burial ground
and tempt history out of its warrens.)*

Not Like Others

I do not write poems like the others.
Perhaps I should.
Others gain accolades.
Perhaps I do write poems like the others.
If you know, please tell me so.
Others do not try to write poems like mine.
Perhaps they choose not to.
Perhaps they cannot.
So many poems, so many poets
in such profusion
confusion
words rhyming and not
cadence even and not
ideas with clarity or not.
Who can know what is right
in an enterprise with no maps or guides?